One Second to Think

One Second to Think

20/20 Mindsight for Your Critical Moments of Brilliance

Leon Quan

iUniverse, Inc.
New York Lincoln Shanghai

One Second to Think
20/20 Mindsight for Your Critical Moments of Brilliance

iUniverse books may be ordered through booksellers or by contacting:

iUniverse
2021 Pine Lake Road, Suite 100
Lincoln, NE 68512
www.iuniverse.com
1-800-Authors (1-800-288-4677)

ISBN-13: 978-0-595-35191-6 (pbk)
ISBN-13: 978-0-595-79887-2 (ebk)
ISBN-10: 0-595-35191-3 (pbk)
ISBN-10: 0-595-79887-X (ebk)

Printed in the United States of America

Contents

Acknowledgments

My first presentation to students took place in 1989 at Villa de Paz K–8 School. Since that time, my life has been an extraordinary adventure upon which I have based this book. Each year that's passed has proven to be a new milestone that has enabled me to communicate with audiences in an ever-changing culture. These real-life chapters are similar in all of us; they are the artwork of the human experience, so I must extend my gratitude to those who have helped me unlock and present the high points of my epic saga.

To my mother, Connie, who has never given up on searching for her passions, voice, music, and true happiness.

To my Aunt Carol and Uncle Terry whose support and encouragement enrich my life in the bad times, as well as the good.

To my grandmother Ruth who has shared the treasure of her perspective and forthrightness.

To my brother Eric and his wife Tina for their gift of "being in the band" when I needed music the most.

To my best friend Steve for pushing to me to speak publicly, rap boldly, recover gently, and live truthfully.

To my wife Lori and her amazing ability to pick out the harmonies in our everyday love song.

Prologue

Snapshots of Peak Performance

It's go time! Adrenalin times ten. I've done this a thousand times. Fear still hovers in the background, hoping his friend Failure will pose an opportunity for him to grow. *Not today, Buddy.* Experience has his say. In this charged moment, the pendulum nears its arc, and time slows. Standing outside double doors and gathering my wits, a practiced composure ushers in a critical second of astute observation. The students trickle in from four entrances; the gymnasium amplifies a feverish hum of anticipation. It's evident in their faces: not everyone is quite sure why they are here. I've already encountered a few skeptical observers. They're adults, maybe administrators or counselors, but most probably, they're teachers. I look around and evaluate the venue—no stage, no theatrical lighting, no huge video screens. Does it get any more challenging than this? One man, one microphone, one message, and 1,800 teenagers. I arrive at myself. My sense of presence seems to accelerate time to its usual pace, and the pendulum begins its downswing. I'm in the zone.

There's no other place the entire student body will fit. Both sides of the gym have become a modern-day Colosseum. The preconceived notions written all over their faces have now melted into an attentive engagement. This hushed audience didn't realize they would laugh so much in the introduction (I caught 'em off guard). Now they're disarmed, interested, and I'm met with a respectful gaze. In the silence from this usually unruly crowd, I discern a hopeful prayer: *Please, just give us something real.* The teachers watching can't believe what they're seeing. The cadence, delivery, and timing of the message have been fashioned for impact, honed over a decade to profound effectiveness. How many sets of adolescent ears have heard and believed? Probably close to a million. This is the moment I've dedicated my life to, the tipping point to the extraordinary. We've all experienced this at one time or another, that pregnant critical second when we decide, *Today everything changes!* As I look each of them in the eyes, I feel the magnitude of my words penetrate their hearts, and the thought hits me: *it's their turn.*

The presentation is coming to a conclusion. As the final words hang in the air, a gasp of gratitude is released. I've given my words of inspiration and my permission: *you can breathe now.* There's a palpable momentum as each of the listeners regards one another. *What did we just experience?* They feel stronger, empowered, and inspired. Some, for the first time in their lives, feel understood and unique. The resounding ovation that follows offers more than a courtesy; it's a personal thank-you for opening the doors of potential and ambition and giving wings to the poetry that was locked inside. A lone student can't contain his enthusiasm within the applause; he shoots to his feet. Another follows from across the gym, then another, and more follow suit. Soon the entire group is locked into a moment of self-affirmation. Their applause is galvanizing a collective moment for themselves. It will live inside them long after they have forgotten my name. The little voice inside my head reminds me, *you chose love*, a reminder that stings my ego for a moment. For a conflicted second, I *want* the adoration. Then I have to let the little voice win. It was never about me; it's about *them*.

My name is Leon Quan. For the last fifteen years, I have been involved in the successful development of youth. My background and education are in religious studies, but my greatest successes have been with secular audiences. I have delivered countless presentations to schools and conferences all over the country and leveraged my skill as a communicator in venues for youth ministry at the local-church and national level, in radio and webcasting, and in concert and music-festival production and promotion. In conjunction with thousands of school assemblies, I've toured and performed in a rap band, consulted law enforcement, lectured graduate students, and trained church youth leaders. Now I am entering a new phase as an author.

In 1999, I started a consulting and professional-speaking company dedicated to empowering the emerging young leaders of America. We poised this company (Quan Presentations) to reach the newly identified millions of younger people who now represent high school and college campuses. They are a market group that generates billions of dollars, and they are the greatest target as an emerging voting constituency. As the perpetuators of pop culture, this age group is setting the tone for a global paradigm.

The book you are reading should be examined in two halves. The first half is to inform the reader about a world of exploitation and profit in which the critical seconds of brilliance and poetry of today's youth are being ripped from their throats before they have an opportunity to be shared. The second half will entertain and inspire as you read and learn from a collection of modern-day *parables of clarity*. In the valuable moments you invest reading, it is my desire that you'll be convinced that your adventure has invited you to jump in, and that as you stand at the threshold, you'll make your choice.

Leon Quan
April 10, 2005
Chandler, Arizona

Introduction

Every day, the headlines remind us of the moments *following* the split seconds that make up the exciting parts of our lives. The drama that galvanizes our experiences is often set against the backdrop of critical seconds. It's said that in the seconds before you die, your whole life passes before you. Moments that wove the tapestry of your days together become magnified, and you are acutely aware of just how

> The greatest wealth, liberty, and happiness will come to those who step forward with insightful composure through overwhelming situations.

significant each minute that passed really was. Time is marked out for us with these tiny increments of meaning, and our greatest lessons are learned in light of their revelations. Those who observe modern life must admit that we are led by the television from sad and depressed to tragic and relieved as a typical daily episode. This process is the strategic capture of the way we think, a mindless substitute for cognitive exercise that helps us cope with all of our fears. When faced with the opportunity to take a smidgen of our own unique life force and implement purpose or significance, most of us cower in the shadow of those who appear to have more composure. My goal for writing this book is to convey the idea that when you take control of the right seconds in your life, you'll reach the highest level of freedom and power. I also want to recognize that the defining moments that allow life to shape you can be split-second miracles that transform your mind. More and more people are searching for the right approach to finding what is becoming the single most difficult state to achieve: clarity.

My hope is that you will not only be enthralled with the stories and insights that I share, but that you will be enthralled with the emergence of your *own* critical moments of brilliance. In this idea lies dominion over our favorite escorts, fear and doubt, and their companions, failure and negativity. In the following pages, you'll hear how people just like you have allowed their critical seconds to destroy them, as well as how your mastery of 20/20 mindsight will profoundly redirect your adventure.

The greatest wealth, liberty, and happiness will come to those who step forward with insightful composure through overwhelming situations. The right action or word or thought at the right moment makes all the difference. I've highlighted quotes, key phrases, and terms that will benefit you if you begin to use them within your paradigm. These words will act like software updates to the mental operating system you're currently using. This new way of observing, examining, and responding in just a second is not new at all. It is actually a streamlined version of the common wisdom taught in all faiths and belief systems. Unfortunately, we can all see that lately there is a gaping hole in our common-wisdom department.

As you begin recognizing these simple approaches, you will undoubtedly become more and more adept with your skills, and this in turn will create a whole new world of opportunities. You'll also start to feel an inner sense of timing that will create urgency for the fruition of your powerful projections. Like a mental tickle or when you finally realize the punch line to a joke, this enthusiastic feeling of awakening is indicative of your true grasp of 20/20 mindsight. Simply put, you won't want to miss a *second* of it!

Chapter One

The Power of Mindsight

The danger of the past was that men became slaves. The danger of the future is that man may become robots.

Erich Fromm

Critical Seconds Can Shape Your Destiny

Throughout history, the most influential thinkers have shaped our world with their unique ability to show us (sometimes in dramatic fashion) that which is locked within all of us. The qualities and characteristics that constitute our individual spirits are the key to touching the divine. So the next most obvious question is, how come we don't all think like Einstein or Da Vinci? Why do we lack the focus of Tiger Woods or Hillary Clinton? How can we perform like Venus Williams, Michael Jordan, or Tom Brady? Well, the answer is that on a biological level we *are* just like the greatest minds of all time. The difference is that these masters of history captured a lightning bolt and rode it—in the form of their acute *mindsight*. At the right time and in the right manner, these brilliant thinkers unleashed the full fury of their intellects and forged their place in history. So *my* question is, where were their heads a second before their peak experience? What tiny piece of preparation can we glean from these great history makers to help us on our own journeys? In my own life, if I could go back to the critical seconds where I made the biggest mistakes, I could keep from hurting myself and others so absentmindedly. If I could change anything, I would not want someone to tell me *what* to think, but *how* to think. Looking back is always clear; looking forward is not so easy.

Seeing Forward

Looking back in history, we see that the great thinkers and doers (I like calling them "life executives") had the unique ability to see forward. They created their worlds from the fantastic visions inside their minds. We can clearly see the fingerprints of excellence all over the works of these timeless masters.

Michelangelo, the brilliant creator of the magnificent statue *David*, is a powerful example of how one mind's projection can take shape in the world of reality. For those of you who are not familiar with this sculpture, it's a breathtaking monument. Standing thirteen feet tall, the statue is carved out of solid marble and pays homage to David, the ancient king of Israel. Not only is it a masterpiece because of the craftsmanship and talent it took to perfectly carve such a sculpture out of stone, but this giant looks as though it might someday come to life—rather than signifying someone who has long been dead. And get this: the entire statue was carved by hand with tools from centuries ago. Now here's the clincher: Michelangelo is quoted as saying that the image of this great piece of art was already in the marble; he just carved away the unneeded rock from the slab of flawed marble that everyone else thought was a gigantic hunk of garbage.

Michael Jordan is the undisputed greatest basketball player of all time. His failures and missed shots have been constantly used as an ode to practice and perseverance. His being cut from his high school team is only one example of Jordan's tenacity. Still, the reason we talk about him today is for the many times the ball was put into his hands and he shocked the world with his game-winning ability. His split-second agility and composure are unmatched. Whenever a game comes down to the final second—for any team and for any star player—spectators are reminded of Michael Jordan. Jordan is a master of critical seconds. His mind has never been locked in by the static drawings of a playbook or by the precedents of style and execution created by players who went before him.

Royce Gracie is one of the world's greatest martial artists. He is the only no-holds-barred fighter to ever successfully defeat four fighters in one night. At only 178 pounds, Gracie consistently wins against fighters that outweigh him by fifty pounds or more. Almost every facet of the military's Special Forces and law enforcement has adopted the Brazilian fighting style that has made him famous. The world would never have known about Brazilian jujitsu unless the Gracie family had believed enough to share it.

In 1984, eighteen-year-old Royce Gracie came to the United States to live with his brother Rorian. Both brothers had studied jujitsu under their father, Helio, who had developed a whole new style in Brazil. Believing that their fighting technique was superior, they taught martial arts from their garage to whoever would learn. Some days they would teach and train for up to ten hours. For ten years, the Gracies would train and teach without any backing or sponsorship. In 1993, they finally opened their first school.

In order to present the effectiveness of this new Brazilian jujitsu and to promote their school, the Gracies created a new tournament-style event called the Ultimate Fighting Championship. The UFC presented fighters from every discipline in a battle octagon to compare different fighting styles in real combat. Without knowing who would come to fight, the Gracies gambled that their style would prevail against any opponent. Warriors from every walk of life came to UFC to compete. Many of the competitors were champions from around the globe who had dominated in previous matches. With unwavering confidence, twenty-six-year-old Royce Gracie stepped into the octagon and literally choked three champion challengers into submission in one night!

The Gracies had an uncanny vision of the future. Armed with only their belief in their chosen artistry, they made concerted efforts and walked straight into their own legend. They possessed the ability to see forward and create a world from the pictures in their heads. Through the power of their *mindsight*, they shaped their destiny.

Chapter Summary

The great minds of past and present are examples that we all have the capability to create our own world with *mindsight*. Critical seconds of clarity precede masterful execution.

Who are the examples you look to for inspiration?

Why are their stories interesting to you?

Have you discovered your purpose for greatness?

Name five goals you have that could change your world.

1.

2.

3.

4.

5.

Chapter Two

Harnessing the Moment
of Action

One secret of success in life is for a man to be ready for his opportunity when it comes.

Benjamin Disraeli

Awaken

There is a powerful and defining moment within every person's life. It is the magical instant that will either make or break an individual's destiny. When we see the mistakes of our past, many of us cling to the notion that we would not change anything that may have happened. Those experiences were great teachers to us, and, even though some of them were painful, we can see their value now. But what if we could see the future? How many of us would walk headlong into calamity? All of the zeal for learning through mistakes would melt into excitement for the opportunity to capitalize on knowledge of events to come. We'd be out buying lottery tickets if we had that secret combination of numbers before anyone else. We'd invest in the stock market if we knew that our values would compound. We'd buy the best and most stylish clothing, purchase the sickest toys, and travel around the globe if we were sure that our incomes would support our lifestyles. If we saw ourselves making mistakes, most of us would do our best to avoid the pitfalls. Well, we *can* live this kind of life—if we want to.

The power we posses to create this reality is locked inside our minds. I'm constantly amazed at how many people spend so much of their time insulating themselves against trouble and tragedy, neglecting the power they posses to create the world they desire. Every day we are bombarded with messages from advertisers to take action to utilize our creative power. They spend millions to convince us that the second we take action, our lives will get easier. They tell us all the features and benefits of their product and explain in vivid detail how, after we act, it's all smooth sailing from there…until tomorrow, when the whole process starts over.

Basic sales fundamentals give us a tiny glimpse into the human thought process. The best sales teachers in the world constantly remind us of a single critical moment. This moment is referred to as the "closing moment." It occurs the second after the salesman asks you to purchase the product. It is that heavy second when we tend to cover the silence with comfortable conversation. The rule of sales is, "the first one who talks owns it." The key idea here is that, in our everyday lives, there are people who understand how profound it is to *anticipate* the moment of action.

Doctors explain the biological changes in our bodies as we experience the adrenaline rush that occurs when we take action and buy something. Some people are even addicted to the feeling they get when they shop or gamble. Both activities require us to take action with our money. The top billionaires in the world report feelings of excitement when they make huge investments that are filled with risk. How can we take the power of our critical moment and harness its creative energy? How do we know when our million-dollar second has arrived?

For the millions of people who would like to take control over their ad-saturated minds, for the thousands who don't want to keep trying to keep up with the hyperspeedy infomercial roller coaster, for the youth of America who want to

reclaim their sanity from two-second TV frame programming, now is the time to implement a "one-second-to-think"
rule. **Rule:** Every day and in all of your actions, commit yourself to vigilantly taking inventory of your critical seconds.

Recognize

The first step in mastering your mindsight is the recognition that your weakness to negative impulses is a learned
behavior. Your immersion in a culture of buying, consuming,
internalizing, and identifying demands your total submission.
Let me say this as succinctly as possible: in the advertising
world, your value as a
human being is depend-
ent only on your mind-
less buying action and
your disposable income.

> In the advertising world, your value as a human being is totally dependent on your mindless buying action and disposable income.

When it comes to engaging with those out there who only
want you to act within their context, it's critical that you see
through this insidious plot to steal your money by selling you
your identity. You heard me right. Most of the time when we
spend money, we are not buying products; we are buying the
thing that most defines us in our mind. The worst kind of follower is the one who blindly regurgitates the manipulative
sound bites they have been spoon-fed. In what ultimately
takes only a moment, many people change the course of their
destiny with a split-second hope to find themselves.

Using Your "Actor"

Well, I know many of you reading are now saying to yourselves, "that sounds easy enough," and in some ways I'm trying to simplify. But the truth is that we all fall victim to this relentless onslaught on our "actor." I use the term "actor" in lieu of the general term for our brain, which is "thinker." While the title of the book seems intrinsically connected to *thinking*, the byproduct of the book will hopefully be to help with a change in *action*. Here lies all the fun! When you reclaim the power you posses (that so many others recognize you have), you begin your journey of exerting influence over your world in what amounts to be just seconds. You can instantaneously draw people and prosperity to you through words and deeds, and you can have control over the momentum of your life. You can feel the sense of significance and empowerment that we all have forfeited at one time or another. To harness the lucid moments of truth within our relatively short existence is the whole reason we're living.

Respond

Now here is where this book begins to relieve some readers with an admonition to stop reading if they're feeling skeptical. Why? Because at this point we're going to start assuming a few things about those who want to take action for themselves. The first assumption is that there are positive and negative people in the world, and those who read on must have some iota of positivity. Second, if you have ever tried to talk some people out of their fatal negativism, then you know it's got to be a choice that they make on their own. This book will not be a long attempt at trying to convince those eternally negative skeptics that they should abandon their totally irrational vice grip on everything that's bad in the world. I can't stand when brilliantly executed motivational and inspirational messages are picked apart by people who feel the need to harness their critical seconds to tear down what they *refuse* to believe. What I mean is that some people will just never get it! So if that's you, then your response should be to hand this book to someone who is really optimistic about life. Of course that person won't appreciate your gift; they'll never repay you. After all, you spent some money on this book, and it's really probably not worth the effort. See what I mean?

For those of us who will be tracking along together for a bit, here's the deal. This whole book revolves around your ability to act. Start right now by beginning to consider some of those blank and unaccounted-for seconds in your day. What happens to the lost increments of time that whiz through our minds when we don't realize it? It's these undisciplined moments that fade our discretion and blunt our wise and compassionate acuity. Your commitment to identifying your transitional seconds and taking the reins back from the con men of your subconscious is the gateway to mastering the mindset of impulse management.

Chapter Summary

When you encounter your defining moments, can you recognize how they will affect your future?

Have you recalled a time in your life in which your decisions made a drastic difference on the outcome for yourself or others?
   List examples: _____

_____

_____

How will you begin to anticipate your moments of decision?

The first step to acting upon your brilliant moments of clarity is accounting for all of your undisciplined time. Can you identify some times in your everyday routines that could be reclaimed?
   List examples: _____

_____

_____

Chapter Three

Pop Culture Savvy

Don't confuse fame with success. Madonna is one; Helen Keller is the other.

Erma Bombeck

There are many people in the world who realize the benefits and power of *your* critical moments. They would like to capitalize on them if you let them. Every day, you and I are baptized in a sea of persuasive messages that make us act, move, and buy. These messages exalt the stupid and make the ignorant an alarming norm. We're told that we are too fat and too slow, unstylish and uneducated, vitamin deficient and we have slip-

> **Information is power.**

ping memories. Pundits preach fear and suggest that our own neighborhoods are dangerous places that we should be scared of. If we didn't exercise some amount of discretion concerning what we believe and what we discard or de-emphasize, we would be in a constant state of unrest, trying to untangle our jumbled minds. The reason this problem exists is that information is power. With broad strokes of creative advertising, it's now possible to spend millions of dollars on the message and reap billions of dollars on the product.

In years past, our world was shaped by the people with the most influence in our lives. These are people who actually had a stake in our success—people who were emotionally vested. Parents, pastors, community leaders, and teachers were the weightiest voices of wisdom. Now another age is dawning, and it's becoming clear that the influences we used to depend on are being drowned out by five hundred channels of infomercial morality. Both women and men are now being measured with an impossible standard for their body image. Our values, standards of behavior, and concern for our world are being molded to the will of those who don't care about us. The insight we've gained into the human mind reveals a million-dollar secret. If you can get someone's attention for *one second*, they will act at your command. As humans, we have a mindless tendency to follow the ones who simply move. Sometimes, it doesn't even matter in what direction. This phenomenon reflects whatever herdlike mentality enabled Gary Dahl, the inventor of the Pet Rock, to become rich.

Gary Dahl, a California advertising man, was having drinks with his buddies one night in April 1975, when the conversation turned to pets. As a lark, Mr. Dahl informed his friends that he considered dogs, cats, birds, and fish to all be pains in the neck. They make a mess; they misbehave; they cost too much money. He, on the other hand, had a pet rock, and it was an ideal pet—easy and cheap—and it had a great personality. His buddies started to riff with the off-the-wall idea, and pretty soon they were all tossing around the notion of a pet rock and all the things it was good for.

Dahl spent the next two weeks writing the *Pet Rock Training Manual*, a step-by-step guide to having a happy relationship with your geological pet, including instructions for how to make it roll over and play dead and how to housebreak it. "Place it on some old newspapers. The rock will never know what the paper is for and will require no further instruction." To accompany the book, Dahl decided to actually create a pet rock. He went to a builders supply store in San Jose and found the most inexpensive rock in the place—a Rosarita Beach stone—which was a uniform-size, rounded gray pebble that sold for a penny. He packed the stone in excelsior in a gift box shaped like a pet carrying case, accompanied by the instruction book.

The Pet Rock was introduced at the August Gift Show in San Francisco (the gift market is much easier to break into than the cutthroat toy market), and then in New York City. Neiman Marcus ordered five hundred. Gary Dahl sent out homemade news releases of himself accompanied by a picture that showed him surrounded by boxes of his Pet Rocks. *Newsweek* did a half-page story about the nutty notion, and by the end of October, Gary Dahl was shipping ten thousand Pet Rocks every day. He appeared on *The Tonight Show, twice.* By Christmas, when two and a half tons of rocks had been sold, three-fourths of all the daily newspapers in America had run Pet Rock stories, often including Gary Dahl's tongue-in-cheek revelations about how each rock was individually tested for obedience at Rosarita Beach in Baja, Mexico, before being selected and boxed. A million rocks sold for $3.95 apiece in just a few months, and Gary Dahl—who decided from the beginning to make at least one dollar from every rock—had become an instant millionaire.

Dahl quit his job in advertising and formed Rock Bottom Productions, and two years later he was interviewed by Don Kracke, inventor of Rickie Trickie Sticky bathroom appliqués, for Mr. Kracke's book *How to Turn Your Idea into a Million Dollars.* Dahl confided to Kracke, "I've got four more ideas.

Wait till you see 'em!" We have been unable to determine if any of the four ideas have seen the light of day.*

* Jane Stern & Michael Stern, *Encyclopedia of Pop Culture* (New York: Harper Perennial Press, 1992).

Virtueless Reality

In June of 2003, the Federal Communications Commission (FCC) attempted to deregulate the rules governing the ownership of media outlets. This decision sparked a fiery debate that is being contested in the Supreme Court even now (summer 2005). Why would all of the billionaire media moguls care about such a change in policy? This shift would allow for historic changes to take place within our most trusted source of information: the news. If this deregulation takes place, it will become legal for gigantic corporations to buy up all the outlets for trusted information and spoon-feed the masses *their* agenda. Never in history has information been so readily available and so powerfully effective at controlling people.

The media megamergers we so ignorantly dismiss from the headlines are not about rich guys making deals. These stories are about the increased efforts to control every niche in the marketplace. A monopoly is a business that owns the entire breadth of a given market; it's illegal to operate one. With the advent of the information age, we've discovered a new truth: the marketplace exists within the categories of our minds. You no longer need to get into your car and drive to the store. The store is in your mind, and the gateway to the market is your personal computer or your television. Long before consumers get to, we won't say "the marketplace," but where the actual transactions are executed, they have already experienced the powerful impulses that lead them to act. This is one of the reasons that we see corporations moving toward a conglomerate-style ownership of every facet of thought. Pop culture is a scary example of how this works.

In a 2001 *Frontline* documentary entitled *The Merchants of Cool,* the producers show a dramatic example of how *everything* concerning advertising to teens and young adults originates from only five or six huge corporations. Young people, the ones characterized in history as idealistic and passionate, are now a market niche that makes up a $175 billion industry. That's right, billion! Even more alarming is how advertisers have discovered that in order to effectively reach young people, they must infiltrate the inner sanctum of youth life. This means doing everything they can to privately study the most candid moments of our adolescence. They've discovered that young people, who are reaching out for their identities, will passionately internalize the products that make up their world. The products become part of their story, like people or places are. So the most effective strategies are the ones that create a symbiotic relationship between person and product. The companies and the young people need each other for the story to be complete. "Do the Dew," "the Pepsi Generation," "the Real Thing," and "Lucky You" are all examples of this sort of tactic.

Seduced Then Sucker Punched

The new millennium has also introduced us to a new definition of glamour and fame. To be famous used to require some form of distinguishing talent. Not anymore. Every manner of perversion is now given a stage to present itself. Being famous is now dangerously confused with being shockingly noticed. Our obsession with seeing our own faces on the television and computer screen has given birth to

> Just because the Internet has provided a cyber reality where the collective brain of mankind can be explored, does that mean we should throw open every dark closet hidden in the cyber psyche?

reality programming. Now, I'm not bad-mouthing the compelling stories that have kept Americans glued to their favorite guilty pastime. Some of the stuff is brilliant. I'll admit that I've enjoyed watching *real* people participate in these fabricated scenarios. In the next decade, I'm making a prediction that these programs will define much of the early twenty-first century. However, just as compelling as how this revolution of the real has drawn us in are the lingering questions about how real we want it to get. Just because the Internet has provided a cyber reality in which the collective brain of mankind can be explored, does that mean we should throw open every dark closet hidden in the cyber psyche? When the fun and titillation we scandalously experience while watching others humiliate themselves comes to us at the expense of *our* dignity, will the line have been crossed? Joseph Francis may answer that question.

At thirty-two, he's already worth one hundred million dollars. He's a self-made media mogul. As a regular at all the hottest night clubs in the world, Francis capitalized on a secret that everyone knew but that no one had yet exploited: drunken girls do stupid things. Jaunting around on private jets and living a fabulous life of riches and wealth, he is the world's most famous sexual predator. Joseph Francis is the founder of the *Girls Gone Wild* video series. As he travels the globe, Francis and his camera crew search for inebriated girls who will expose themselves for party trinkets or small amounts of cash. Now this may sound harmless enough; the girls are all consenting adults, right? Wrong. Francis has been repeatedly indicted for filming underage girls. In addition to rape and drug charges, he has also been ordered to repay $1.1 million after it was discovered that he had made unauthorized charges to the credit cards and checking accounts of people who had ordered his videos. Still, Francis is not viewed as a menace to society. Among the young celebs of today's Hollywood, he has become a modern-day version of Hugh Hefner. His seemingly distasteful exploitation of young girls is overshadowed by his wealth and proximity to the famous.

Paris Hilton could have leveraged her influence, wealth, and family reputation to establish herself as an American version of royalty. As heir to the Hilton Hotel conglomerate, she is worth billions of dollars. She instead has chosen to embody the appearance of absolutely careless indulgence. Being known as a party girl and a spoiled socialite brat enabled Paris to launch a TV show and a modeling career. Her party life, though, was crashed in 2004 when an ex-boyfriend (Rick Soloman) released an explicit tape over the Internet of the two having sex in a hotel room. He reportedly disavowed himself of the initial release of the footage, but then he licensed and sold his copy of the tape and made *seven million dollars*! I believe Paris Hilton has a long life ahead of her, and I also believe she will probably do some outstanding things with her fortune, but that tape will *never* go away. Twenty years from now, she may have given her entire fortune to the poor (I know, I know; it's just an example), but the headlines will still read, "Former Porno Brat Gives Away Cash."

May millions of middle school girls read this paragraph and whisper a silent prayer of relief: "Thank God I'm *not* Paris Hilton."

Franchising the Teen Experience

In an interview with movie star Leonardo DiCaprio following the filming of the movie *The Beach*, DiCaprio told reporters about his time in Bangkok, Thailand. When questioned about the uniqueness of the life and culture of the people of Thailand, the star laughed and explained how his visit had lacked much mystery due to the fact that Bangkok has been taken over by American pop culture. He went on to explain that many of his travels to foreign destinations were now this way. Which Starbucks or McDonald's would you like to see?

So it would seem that the term "pop culture," short for popular culture, implies that the masses or population are all taking part in worldwide trends. Advertisers predicate their campaigns on a powerful perception that everyone is somehow connected with their product. Those who are not involved lack tremendous portions of what the rest of the world already knows. But wait; upon further examination, we see something else underneath the hype. The very same people telling us that the world is outpacing us in fashion and fun are studying us closely and focusing their message at smaller and smaller groups of consumers. The marketing strategies used on youth only a generation ago are now narrowing the approach down to the two- and four-year intervals between ages ten and twelve (tweens) and between ages twenty-five and twenty-nine. The end result is a marketing message that reads like this:

"Every twelve-year-old in the world knows about this product and is using it right now…except you. We all share the same attitude, and we are cool. If you participate with us, you can become cool too. However, you must get the product *now* or face the consequence of being an outcast." Silly isn't it?

In my travels as a speaker and consultant all over the United States, I have encountered this recurring theme derived from

the mentality of pop culture. Youth from the most rural agricultural areas work extremely hard to emulate the youth in
vibrant metropolitan cities as portrayed on television and in
movies. With the exception
of their proximity to events
ingrained in their geogra-
phy (e.g., rodeos, state and
county fairs, agricultural
cycles), young people are
doing their best to look

> If students only knew how
> their passionate pursuit of rel-
> evance and significance was so
> irrelevant and insignificant to
> the people selling them their
> identities.

almost exactly alike. It's funny and disturbing at the same
time to hear the same story from rural New Mexico and rural
Wyoming. Youth drive for hours to the nearest mall where
there is a Gap store. Advertising for the Gap is a brilliant
example of creating a unisex fashion for all types of people. It
has the widest penetration into vast portions of Middle
America. Students in cities with more malls and choices view
the Gap as just another option for clothing, while students
from rural areas view it as their only means of connection to
the rest of the world. Many celebrities and musicians have
also adopted this cross-cultural/cross-gender approach to
fashion. If you turn down the sound to CMT, MTV, or VH1,
you will not know what kind of music is being played. Now,
you might say, "Leon, let's all unite under this one banner of
prudent and wonderfully moderate clothing!" Even though I
do love their cargo pants, and they do provide that twenty-
nine-inch inseam I need for my short legs, here's what I think

we should recognize: the purpose of downplaying the difference in age and gender is *exploitation and profit*!

The big con here is that not only are we are being told how to *find* ourselves and *be* ourselves, but from the business standpoint of these shrewd clothiers, they would like to convince us that cheaply made casual wear in a few different colors defines our social standing and value too. I do not find fault with the clothing makers; I find the fault in the efforts of advertisers to galvanize the segments and differences in the young in order to make money, and in the fact that they do this by making us all look the same. If students only knew that their passionate pursuit of relevance and significance was irrelevant and insignificant to the people selling them their identities.

When marketing to the young, males are labeled *mooks*, and females, *midriffs*. Both terms carry a definition that is totally engrained in a negative stereotype. Advertisers are the only ones in society who can get away with this sort of class/gender/race segregation. If you buy into any of this kind of hogwash to define yourself, then you might as well check everything that is sacred to you at the door. To state it plainly, if we continue to leave the character-modeling aspects of life to pop culture, young people won't even have the option to define themselves in any positive, self-conscious, and inspired way.

There is no mainstream media outlet that has founded itself on the principles of youth development and individual leadership and thought. Why? Because there is no money in that! The rich guys can't fill their pockets with money made from inspiration and character when there is so much more profit in burning a larger hole in our collective cerebral ozone. The end result is what we see each day on our campuses all across the country—burned out, hopeless students who have adopted a jaw-dropping audacity that tells them that the people who have the greatest devotion to them (parents, teachers, and community leaders) are in their lives for comedic relief. Adults are the dopey, irrelevant support staff in the grand stage of these youth's sitcom lives. Any time an adult steps forward with a message of caution and wisdom, that adult is quickly dismissed with a marginalizing proclamation like "boring" or "I know, I know!" The fact is that these youth *don't know*, and that is why we have to embrace some new assumptions about pop culture.

Assumption 1: Pop-culture advertising is not art. It is a skill that has created many millionaires. It takes talent and creativity, but true art draws upon the virtues and immortal characteristics of mankind. No matter how creative and novel this sort of advertising is, *it does not define us.* If we forfeit our brains to the advertisers, we will be handing over all the true genius in life to William Hung. "AI" means *American Idol* to the world of pop culture, but in the scientific world it refers to the term "artificial intelligence." If we don't see through this ploy, we are destined to buy beer from Jesus and car insurance from the Dalai Lama.

Assumption 2: Pop culture does not deserve our focus. Like a willful mental glaucoma, pop culture slowly invades the scope of our vision until we are totally blind. This happens all in the name of mild entertainment. It does not rise to such a level of importance that we should strive desperately to fit into it. The perceived fear that a few simpletons might judge our appearance is a never-ending hamster wheel. If you don't look away now and begin the arduous process of seeing the world through your own eyes, your entire meaning in life will be the profit margin on some rich guy's ledger.

Assumption 3: Pop culture is not based in truth. Brian Warner (aka Marilyn Manson) said it best in the award-winning documentary *Bowling for Columbine*: "This culture is based in fear and consumption." If everything that is thrown at you is true, then you are ugly, fat, and poor, and the best you can hope for is to be selected for the next reality show to make you over. Do not trade your dignity for an airbrushed version of life in which the most defining moment for you will be the last episode of *Friends*.

Your mind is a gateway to endless possibilities and tremendous wealth and freedom. Your eyes are the entry. The greatest power any person or corporation can have over you is in the subtle suggestion that you should cover your eyes with the lenses of their choosing. These lenses will bend your sight in the direction they choose, thus relieving you of your power and individuality. They will define you for their world and relegate you to the obscure masses of unknown and long-dead peasants. In a thousand years, when the explorers of tomorrow dig us up, it will be clear that millions upon millions of prosperous Americans claimed their place in history in front of a TV, taking part in the programming—not by determining the lineup of shows to be presented, but as victims of the act of controlling those who resigned their minds. Stale and stagnant, the final condition of a generation that has more ability to be brilliant, passionate, and creative than any previous generation is that of halitosis of the soul. You have control over your mind. If you want to develop sharp focus and mental clarity, if you want to lead and be different, if you want your life to have significance now, you must learn the secrets to having 20/20 mindsight.

Chapter Summary

Can you identify how pop culture identifies the world around you?

List examples: _____

_____

_____

Which outlets for crucial information do you trust now?

Which outlets for crucial information will you trust in the future?

Do you think that Joe Francis and Paris Hilton have any real influence on society?

Whose opinion of you (outside of your own) really matters?

Chapter Four

Feeding Your Mindsight

We do not have to visit a madhouse to find disordered minds; our planet is the mental institution of the universe.

Johann Wolfgang von Goethe

Now, hopefully I've got you thinking. I hope you want to break free of the grasp of common thought. The hardest part about the next segment will be the seemingly painful withdrawal from satisfying our mental addiction to the constant saturation of our every thought. Unconsciously we have practiced the habit of filling our minds with a never-ending stream of meaningless information. The easiest and most pleasurable part of a pop-culture lifestyle is allowing someone else to do all the thinking. Rather than pointing the mind to its most fantastic capabilities, we've allowed our world's pushiest salespeople to choke the poetry from our innermost being. In the next segment, we'll introduce two simple and easy habits into our everyday routines. Although the suggestions I offer will seem to some a little humorous, I am dead serious about the effectiveness of the techniques.

The Discipline of Silence

In every culture since the dawn of civilization, mankind has found the strength to carry on in the face of impossible circumstances. Where does the courage to sail into the unknown come from when everyone around you is telling

> Be quiet for one second!

you that you will fall off the edge of the earth? What part of our brain tells us that the moon is a destination, when for thousands of years we considered it a god, a shrine, or a symbol, but not a place we could go? What possesses us to strap rockets to our vehicle and light the fuse? Where are the concepts of behemoth skyscrapers and titanic cruise liners born? Before any of the remarkable achievements of man ever become realities, they are ideas, momentary strokes of genius originating in the birthplace of fantasy. Then, for the process of creating, a subsequent uninterrupted flow of thought is needed to unfold the majestic rationality required to execute the vision.

All people have the potential to give birth to an idea or an approach that changes the current state of mankind. More specifically, *you* have the potential to add something revolutionary to your world. But in a world predicated on free enterprise, you always have to contend with the competition. What I mean is that there is profit in ideas. You must have the right timing and the ability to communicate how your brilliance can benefit people. Choose not to follow this advice, and someone else will find a way to steal your concept. So how do you tap the realm of greatness? First, be quiet for one second. It's unfortunate that what sounds so simple is actually the toughest thing to achieve in our updated modern lives. Every day we experience an abortion of brilliance due to the unending drone of constant mental noise. It's obvious that we hate the sound of our own thoughts. Creating images in our minds is better left to the little dots that make up our television pictures.

Opportunities to bring forth your next great idea will come naturally to your mind if you only let them. The brain is an active organ. It continues to conjure images and devise dreams and schemes even when you sleep. This is the major premise behind hypnotism. Suggestive influence perpetrated on a vulnerable brain can border on mind control. Young people of the world allow themselves to be controlled and hypnotized by not guarding their independent thoughts.

My messages to schools and conferences all over the country revolve around this theme: think for yourself! Right here, right now, commit yourself to finding your voice and your way and your truth. It's there, but you must make it emerge. Your choice to take control of your thoughts will prove difficult, maybe even painful, but imagine the pain of regret if you don't. Imagine living a long life and only at the end discovering that there was so much more than what was being portrayed in life's sound bytes. What places would you travel to? What people would you meet? What great undertakings would you have your name attached to if only you had believed in the power of your own voice? You will never hear that voice unless you take one second and listen.

The following is a list of times that you should start allowing your inner sense of direction to guide you through a simple second of silence. This list is for real people, busy people who live in an occupied, jumbled, senseless, and sometimes-overwhelming world. These moments are suggested to create a foot in the doorway of your thoughts, and I believe that what lies beyond that door is the greatest adventure you'll ever know. Before I relay them to you, though, I must first give you the premise on which your thoughts should originate.

When starting the process of independent thinking, dictate for yourself the three most important priorities you embrace. These priorities are the place that all your thoughts can come back to at any time and you will feel no conflict about their validity. For each person these priorities will be different, but the outcome will be the same. For me these priorities are as follows: my inner sense of truth and my adherence to that sense, my family and their well-being, and my expression of these passions to the world around me. It is now my choice as to whether I will allow these priorities to be enriched in absent moments (like in front of the TV) or whether they will be neglected in favor of mental junk food. Now, in one epic moment of silence, I can commit to feeding the brilliant, creative, and passionate components of my life in the critical seconds that most people waste.

1. **Driving:** Most people will spend one third of their life behind the wheel of a car. In your first dramatic effort to take the mental reins from "the idiot makers," execute one trip in your car in silence, with only your thoughts. It will feel absolutely unnatural the first time you do it, but the ideas you'll conceive in that time will pay big returns.

2. **In the shower or on the toilet:** No, I'm not kidding. The most honest genius will have to admit that brilliance arrives in the most unexpected moments. Start looking for this phenomenon, and I guarantee you'll see it's true.

3. **Right before bed:** In the bathtub or lying in bed before you fall asleep is a strategic time when your relaxed mind can arrive at valuable solutions.

4. **During your dreams:** When moments of perfect clarity arise within you, it may sometimes be a gift from your subconscious. Keep a pad of paper or a tape recorder next to your bed for these idea deliveries. You may awaken to a senseless abstract poem, or you may get the answer you've been trying to find.

5. **In a planned time of meditation and reflection:** Consider keeping a regular date with your brain. Allow it to perform its vital function just as you would allow your stomach to digest food before swimming. When you give yourself time to think, you allow your whole body to prioritize the goals you'd like to achieve.

6. **When you're used to doing something else:** If you regularly spend extended time in front of the TV, surfing the Internet, or playing video games, just stop! Throw your brain a curveball and take dominion over your intellect. Control the unnerving compulsion to set blank moments up on intellectual autopilot. When you can master every second with useful engagement, ideas will have a chance to surface.

The list sounds easy, doesn't it? Well try it. You'll quickly experience the habitual mental slavery that we constantly subjugate ourselves to. Try it for one month, every day, and I'll bet you'll see vast improvement in a wide array of areas in your life. Want a raise at your job? Want to find a better job? Want to improve your key relationships? Want to find the discipline to successfully lose weight, exercise, study, write, or create? All the best you have to offer is unlocked in your moments of silence. Those moments are yours; don't give them away! Invest them wisely, and all the wonderful treasures the world has to bestow will surely become your opportunity.

The second basic approach to feeding your mindsight is the simple act of strategic reading. In the 1950s, the United States was right on the verge of a technological monsoon that would last for twenty-five years. This golden quarter-century offered us gigantic leaps forward in the everyday luxuries of air-conditioning, basic kitchen appliances, and the impregnation of our households with sources of information. This revolution was the premise for saying that our society had moved into the information age.

We were told that all the modern conveniences we had developed would offer us ease and comfort and most importantly relief from the daily grind. In

> We will continue to speed up our perceptions of life as fast as our life can be perceived.

theory, we would all be able to spend more quality time doing productive things. The end result, however, revealed something we never anticipated. Human beings by nature tend to work very hard to fill their time occupying their minds. It's true that if we plucked someone out of the 1950s and gave him all the advancements of today, he might enjoy the extra hours afforded him by a dishwasher or washing machine and dryer, or he might enjoy grocery shopping on the Internet, but that's not the world we've evolved into.

The advancements we've experienced have created shifts in how we spend our time. Our actions have now become a reflection of how fast and remarkably our brains can function. Life and experience has been accelerated to match our appetites for information. To state it plainly, we will continue to speed up our perceptions of life as long as the speed at which life can be perceived increases. The power will thus reside with those who can deliver to the brain pictures and symbols that induce desires and actions the quickest. Sex, greed, and hunger essentially drive everyone. Appeal to the worst aspects of human nature, and watch the dollars start rolling in.

So how do we break free? The act of strategic reading is the calculated slowing down our mind needs to develop wisdom. Hand yourself the gifts of prudence and discretion by breaking down the process by which your mind acts. It's much harder for someone to deceive and manipulate you if you are deciphering messages line by line in print.

Rules of Reading

Begin this action today. Again, from the premise of your most important priorities, choose reading material that you know expresses all aspects of an issue. Recognize the tone and

the angle that the author uses to convince you. Commit yourself to reading more than one source before you forge your
opinion about an issue. Nothing important can be summed
up in a one-liner, bumper sticker, or sound byte. Don't let
yourself be relegated to one side of the issue or another. This,
too, is a ploy to give you only two choices; you may be neutral
or indifferent, and that is your choice. Notice that anything
aimed at adults that has lots of pictures is most likely slanted
toward the consumer in you. Read it for fun, but realize it's a
brain Twinkie.

I often encounter people who tell me that they are "just not
a reader." Usually it's in a whiney, complaining voice. These
are the people who try to cloak their lazy brains in the rationality that they are "visual" or "auditory" learners. No kidding!
Everyone is a visual and auditory learner. Babies are visual
and auditory learners. What sets apart infants and adults is
our ability to read. We all love the ready-made imagery that
the TV serves up right at our fingertips. It's easy and requires
no effort from us. But when we focus our mind's efforts on
active and strategic reading, we give wings to our mental
capabilities.

Like a high-performance
foreign sports car, we allow
our brilliance to open the
throttle on the autobahn of
our creativity. When we

> To lock your mind into the context of a plugged-in reality is a prison where you willingly serve your sentence.

allow pop culture to limit the pictures we see in our mind, we stop the process of mental conjuring. Your brain will always fashion your internal ideas in more vivid and vibrant detail when it creates them from scratch. To lock your mind into the context of a plugged-in reality is to lock yourself in a prison where you willingly serve your sentence. You must feed your mindsight enough to grow beyond the contextual walls of pop culture.

Moments of Decision

The final key to feeding your mindsight is control over *your* moment of *decision*. Once you've read and meditated on the ideas that define your world, you will sprint past the majority of people if you will just *make up your mind!* Most people find it much easier to never express a well-thought-out opinion. However, when you look a little closer, the main reason is that they don't have a clue what they're talking about. They are regurgitating some half story that was shot out in a forty-five-second news clip. All people have the tendency to bolster their own importance by trying to appear informed. When you stop for a moment and evaluate what is being said, though, very little has any substance. No thought or study was invested.

Chapter Summary

In this chapter, there are six times suggested for reflective thought. Which opportunities could you incorporate into your thought life?

List examples: _____

_____

_____

What are your uncomplicated thought priorities?

How do these guiding priorities shape your perspective?

Right now, make some commitments for reading books that specifically challenge you to think.

List the books you'll read: _____

_____

_____

Are you aware of your moments of decision? Begin to acknowledge every time you make a decision and how you were convinced to do so.

List examples: _____

_____

_____

Chapter Five

Meeting Others with Mindsight

In everyone's life, at some time, our inner fire goes out. It is then burst into flame by an encounter with another human being. We should all be thankful for those people who rekindle the inner spirit.

Albert Schweitzer

The most powerful multiplier of 20/20 mindsight is the magic synergy created when two or more great intellects join forces toward a goal. Every single instance of noteworthy action in our world is hinged upon our ability to act collectively. We put heroes on pedestals, but none ever act alone. Somewhere in the underlying story lies another key player, even if it's just the lowly guy who writes the story down. So how do we find the key players to our story? The next chapter will lay out for you the opportunity that awaits those who will create and join teams of brilliant, creative, and passionate people to move mountains and manifest miracles.

Isolation is the norm for more and more young people today. We don't spend nearly as much time outdoors as we once did. Now, I know that I'm going to sound like an old man reminiscing about the good ol' days, but before we had all the technology available to us now, the interactive gaming that youth participated in was truly interactive…with *people*! Now to clarify what I mean. I have no problem with the Internet or with game systems or with TV; I simply want to point out that the isolation that has separated young people of this generation produces the byproduct of entire groups of youth that can't expand their vocabulary or social skills.

Just watch a group of students some day. Don't let them know they are being watched, and see how much sitcom drama they create in their personal lives. Observe how little their interactions seem to reflect real human discourse. The most alarming outcome of this information-age isolation is the fact that millions of young people are adopting their people skills from the programming targeted at their age. Real interactions in a full range of situations are becoming harder to participate in. True human dynamics that create leadership and influence aren't making their way into normal everyday development.

Great leaders and communicators are adept with the subtler working of human behavior, like people's posturing and facial expressions and other nonverbal communication. Without social mixing as a regular part of our intellectual diet, we will continue to hinder our ability to understand how real people live, think, and develop. Also, the first step in conquering a people is to divide them into isolated pockets and feed them the information you want them to believe. Isn't it amazing how we have greater ability to stay connected through our modern technology, yet we feel less community?

The Synergy Secret

When I was fifteen years old back in 1986, I was at the dawn of a whole new era. As a young Asian American, my upbringing in the heart of Phoenix, Arizona, had helped me acquire a taste for an enriching new adolescent expression: rap music! I'm well aware that my readers were probably not previously thinking, "I'll bet Leon Quan loves hip-hop!" Yet, ever since I was fifteen years old, I have written and performed raps of my own. In fact, I have some very impressive video footage of me at twenty-five. At the height of my experience was an opportunity to rap on stage with over two thousand audience members. It was an electrifying few moments during which I felt the euphoric high that hip-hop stars hope to experience at least once in their lives. In one critical moment, in front of a sea of two thousand fans, with the best sound and lighting rig I'd ever performed on, I learned a powerful principle of success. It had begun ten years earlier—long ago, on a campus far, far away.

In 1986, on my high school campus, a new phenomenon had just taken over during our lunch hour. Groups of students, predominantly African Americans, started gathering together in clusters and battling one another with words. I was amazed at the skill and ease with which these lyrical artists painted verbal pictures and wielded vocal swords. It was the birth of rap battles. As a newly emerging trend, rappers found their inspiration from the founders of this new music. LL Cool J and the Beastie Boys, Run DMC and Whodini were launching a musical revolution that rivaled rock and roll. Some said it would never last, but today we see the hip-hop music industry thriving.

As a young Chinese American, I watched with awe and near worship the spectacle that rappers could create. I would sit and listen, and in my alone time, I would secretly write lyrics of my own that I never imagined would be performed. I told myself that it took a "special something" to be able to deliver the lines the proper way and to not make a fool of yourself or look like a poser.

On one particular occasion, I was standing with a friend of mine watching a rap battle during lunch. He, too, loved rap music. We were both mesmerized with the idea of getting up and bustin' a rhyme. As two little white guys, we wanted our piece of the action. At one climactic moment, I couldn't contain my excitement, and I jumped out into the center of the battle and started my lyric:

Gonna have a little party on the microphone,

So if you're not here to rock, then just go home.

I'm half, he's half of this team.

I'm a four-foot rapper, but I reign supreme,

Cuz I'm awesome one; he's awesome two.

We're not conceited, just better than you!

Maybe it was shock, maybe a little surprise, but for whatever reason, my lyrics broke through the ethnic and stereotypic confines for a critical moment, and I was met with a new level of respect and acceptance from the rappers. Most of those guys were authentic urban gangbanger sorts. Now, many young rappers would be content with this experience alone, but I wanted more, and the story was just getting started. You see, this was just the beginning of an adventure that I didn't even know I was going to embark upon.

I wonder how many adventures in our lives are never fully explored due to the limiting idea that we cannot do some things because the rest of the world just can't visualize them. Anyways, on to the good part. Shortly after that event, I shared the story with a friend and mentor of mine. Steve Peebles, someone who has become my lifelong colleague and advisor, was nearly ten years older than me. He listened patiently as I recounted my lyrics and how the guys at school didn't think I was lame. After hearing me out, Steve (a lover of rap as well) said, "Leon, I think you're talented, and I think you have something to offer the world, but I think it will be hard for you to fully realize your best artistry if it all has to happen at school. The world needs people like you, and it is much bigger than just *your* campus. Also, if you really want to stand out, try creating lyrics that are positive and lift people up."

I was truly challenged by these words, and I decided to try his advice. First, I started writing lyrics that didn't use profanity and that had a positive message. This was a tough task! Ask anyone who uses language as an outlet for personal experiences. Poets, musicians, and comedians all understand how tough it is to never use an expletive and still move people; adding cuss words is the easiest way to sharpen your message. So my first obstacle was writing a rap that didn't rely on the standard lyrical content for creating an impact on the listener.

Next, I shared the new lyrics with Steve. He was totally positive and encouraging. He, too, shared some lyrics he had written. I never realized that an old guy (Steve was twenty-five at the time, but that was old to me) could be so talented. He was by far the most talented rapper I had ever met in person. Steve then took the whole idea to the next level. He told me that we had to find an audience for our music, people who would truly appreciate the effort and time we had put into the writing. If we tried to share this with people from school, they would look at it as competition, and the positive message would be lost.

One day, Steve came to my house with the solution. "Let's go to the most desperate places in the city and share our positive message of inspiration through rap!" It took a little convincing, but soon I could see how it would work. We decided that the best place for us to release our talents on the world was...the projects! That's right, the low-income government-subsidized housing in the bad part of town. Now, understand something here. We were not rolling up with huge fanfare, a sound system, and lights for a rap show. We borrowed a small eight-channel PA system and a tape player with some mics, and we drove Steve's 1979 Monte Carlo down to some of the hardest projects in South Phoenix.

When we arrived on a Thursday afternoon, we parked the car and got the speakers and PA system set up. Steve's girlfriend Darlene watched the equipment, and Steve and I went out to canvass the area to invite people to our show. That night, we performed for about 150 men, women, and children right there in the projects of South Phoenix. Slowly we were discovering how powerful the secret of synergy really was. But that's not the end of the story. Steve and I were energized by how our little outreach had gone. We began dreaming of making an album. In the late eighties, there was nothing and no one we could look to for inspiration. No one was doing what we were doing. Getting studio time and the cost of production

were also hindrances that we didn't know how we could overcome. We continued with our miniconcerts for another year,
touring the different projects in Phoenix on Thursday after-
noons. We opened ourselves up to any people who wanted to
come and watch, and we made it our goal to find others who
shared our dreams and wanted to help.

One day, those people arrived. A group of artists, musicians, dancers, and public speakers caught wind of what we
were doing. They began to attend and assist our miniconcerts
in a volunteer capacity. Our concerts grew in size and scope.
We would bring vocalists and drama, feats of strength and
sound and lights. Soon our little dream became a full-stage
presentation. This group of people had money, and they
wanted us to take our show to other housing projects around
the country. In the following months, we traveled to some of
the hardest housing projects in the country—Watts and
Compton in South Central LA, Baltimore and Kansas City,
Milwaukee and Philadelphia. Our dream and our synergy
propelled us to new heights that we never originally understood. We never did get to make that album—we made *two*!
That's right! Two fully completed CDs. Thousands of our
albums are still in circulation today because of the powerful
secret of synergy.

We've received letters from people all over the nation
telling us how we've made a positive impact on their lives.
The right people coming together at the right time can
accomplish way more than only one can by himself.

Brilliant moments are multiplied ten times over when an alliance of clear-minded people is formed. When I look at my story for the first time in written form, I am amazed. What a journey. Still, I can only imagine that far more dynamic people than myself are reading and are wondering right now how their journey will begin.

So how do you know when an adventure of epic proportions is right outside your door? Lucid, critical moments of brilliance that are focused on building the right team can make all the difference. Which people are the right people? Who should you be looking for? Are the people in your life the people who can go to the next level with you? The following are some of the most crucial questions you must ask yourself about meeting the people who will help you shape your destiny.

Four Pointed Questions about Friendship

Question 1: What is the point of your friendships? The simplest question you can ask about the people who surround you is centered on the outcome of the relationship. Why are you friends with them? I know this seems a little discriminatory, but just take a second to examine this idea. When we are young, we tend to find friends in all shapes and sizes. There is an overwhelming pressure to accept all manner of silliness in the name of friendship. A lot of time is wasted getting involved with the temporary drama that some young people drum up to make their lives more thrilling. Many times we choose the "characters" with funny personalities or strange behavior because they are interesting, rather than finding the *character* that identifies someone of strength and intelligence. If more creative and independent thinkers applied a standard to their investments of time and involvement in friendships, they would discover what the ultrawealthy already know and have known for years. Friendships are *alliances* and can last forever. They can become the foundation from which your epic adventure springs. Wealth, happiness, and opportunity all involve the people you're building friendships with now. Don't waste your precious seconds of brilliance on someone who doesn't get it and never wants to.

Question 2: Does your friendship have a direction? After that last question, you're probably thinking I'm telling you to be selfish and shrewd about who you associate with. Well, you're right, to an extent. After more than a decade of helping students find clarity, I wish I could get more people to abandon their meaningless acquaintances with stupidity. But that doesn't mean I think you should find only perfect friends; that would be impossible. It simply means that you should be committed to identifying a direction you want your life to go in, and those people you choose to associate with should be headed in that direction, too. Will you make mistakes? Surely! You will never find perfection in a friendship, but you can embrace a *direction* for your passionate pursuits.

Question 3: Have you mastered the art of collective projection? Your friends and colleagues all create a picture that can be observed at any time. Using the diagram below, you can begin this exercise and start to see what sort of masterpiece your collective associations have

_____

_____ _____

_____shared goals_____

_____ _____

_____

birthed. Using a divider, get your teammates to fill out the picture wheel with their own thought projections, and then see if they match at all.

Question 4: Does your alliance have a message? One of the strongest elements within groups of positive young people today is religion. This book does not embrace any particular faith, but I do want to recognize an aspect of successful thinking that I have found in most communities. When young people decide that their lives are a message to the rest of the world, whether others agree with the message or not, it is extremely influential. It seems that the reverence and sanctity with which these students deliver their message has a powerful effect on the listener. At displays of worship like public prayer or silent, symbolic meetings at a flagpole, every interview I've ever conducted with students who didn't share the same beliefs resulted in expressions of the utmost respect for the believers' courage. Deciding that you would like your life to be a message for all to encounter can create a magnetizing effect that draws others who respect, admire, and share the same beliefs. Some powerful messages to adopt could be "I am a person of character" or "I am an ambitious young climber" or "My life means something important to the world now." All of these messages can be reinforced through your actions and through your relationships. Mark my words; with consistent adherence to your own inner voice, and with the powerful connections you make with like-minded dreamers, you will have a voice and a life that will give you 20/20 mind-sight for your critical moments of brilliance.

Start looking for the brilliant moments of clarity as they apply to your alliances, and you will most definitely see how the course of your life can change for the better. Many times it's hard to see these events unfolding; the cloak of regularity over your life may blunt the dynamic and make it seem like just everyday routine. But you will be able to look over just one year's time, and it will reveal your adventure.

Chapter Summary

Can you identify the people in your life who are positive influences?

Are there people you spend time with who are negative influences?

Name the positives and negatives that help or hinder your critical moments of brilliance:

Positives: _____

_____

_____

Negatives: _____

_____

_____

Are there any themes to your life?

If you were writing the story of your life now, who would play the main supporting roles?

Chapter Six

Leading with 20/20 Mindsight

By three methods we may learn wisdom: first, by reflection, which is noblest; second, by imitation, which is easiest; and third, by experience, which is the bitterest.

Confucius

I wish I could begin this chapter with the encouraging assurance that all the people you encounter from here on out will follow you just because you're a passionate person. But, the truth is, even with the right people and the right idea and even the right time, you will experience turmoil, drama, immaturity, and skepticism at every turn. Some will misperceive you, some will secretly envy your direction and enthusiasm, and some will just stab you in the back because that's human nature. If everyone could have the clarity and courage it takes to be involved in the adventure, we would all be millionaires and kings.

The fact is that there are more mediocre people in the world than there are fantastic dreamers with visions of magnificence. We study the noteworthy souls of generations past, but when you compare the number of great people with the billions of forgotten, nameless peasants whose lives meant nothing to the movement of mankind, you'll see that the easy road is widely traveled. Get my drift? If you're this far into this book, I know you want more. That means you have to become a leader. There is no way around calling attention to yourself for the purpose of making things happen.

When you begin to see the world bending around your desires and goals, you have just become enlightened. You can't go back. The power you possess is 20/20 mindsight. All human endeavors have progressed through this one great realization. It is the one cognitive skill that calls you to the forefront of humankind and demands that your talents be utilized. If you have a message and a direction, if you have found the others around you who feel the same way you do, it's time to start identifying those split seconds in which leadership can make all the difference.

Preparing for That Moment

The idea that leadership is a trait that some people are born with has always been lost on me. You see, at five foot five, I have always had what I believed was an initial struggle getting others to follow my leadership. I have noticed that some people have advantages, like physical attractiveness or height. Those aspects make people want to follow certain stereotypical leaders. But, as time has revealed many things about true leadership, I have seen that this phenomenon is an acquired and practiced skill. Reading books and listening to CDs and tapes does not develop the skills you need to excel.

Only execution of a plan and overcoming all obstacles and objections will make you a better leader. So the most critical moment of all happens right at the beginning when you decide you will not be a spectator anymore. All eyes will be on you. You'll feel the mounting pressure of having others follow you. The weight of their dependence and scrutiny will first seem like a burden, but as your experiences move you forward, you'll begin to feel a new sense of power as you are cloaked in the aura of influence. You will be a doorway for humanity through which people will see the world that you see, and their reality will be tied to your ability to guide them.

Using the Force

Imagine your life as a moving flow; picture your life force taking a direction. Feel the energy that you create when you are in a room with other people. Now, if you're reading this and saying, "I never feel my energy in a room with others, and I don't think they feel it either!" my answer to you is this: your energy is there; you're just not used to noticing it. And you're maybe accustomed to watching others around you and allowing them to dominate the flow of things. If you want to feel the leadership force that you possess, try this little experiment. Begin to notice how your voice sounds in your head. Then say your thoughts aloud in a room while you're all alone. Then try talking unexpectedly in different social situations.

You'll soon realize that the only thing keeping your leadership back is you. Now, understand what I'm saying. I'm not telling you that everyone will begin to heed your will. I'm saying that you will begin to feel the power of your life force. The reality that you experience every day can be altered by you. It's that simple, but just because you can feel your life giving leadership doesn't mean your influence will appear overnight. In the next couple of pages, we're going to define some very elementary principles that you can apply to your critical moments of brilliance. All of your thoughts concerning one second of leadership will be your preparation for the real thing.

The Magic of Rappority

Rappority is the newest key to unlocking the magic of your leadership model. To energize a generation of PlayStation junkies drunk on the wine of pop culture is no small task. How do you get uninvolved people in today's increasingly cynical age to catch the enthusiasm to make a positive change? Does anyone take leadership seriously anymore? The current trend points toward a necessity for more young, creative, independent thinkers.

The Campus

Since most of my work is done on campuses, I decided to make a designation specifically for the people I deal with the most. I also believe that this approach is very effective in such a weird environment. Never in our lives after high school are we packed together in such an intense and hormonally charged sardine-can world.

Great campus cultures are formed through the implementation of peer mediation, an empowered and well-represented student council, and an increased commitment by student leaders to be the eyes and ears of the campus. Why is it so hard to get students to embrace a positive cause? Many adults remember when positive programs for young leaders created their own self-perpetuated momentum. Now we see the jaded roll of the eyes, the I-don't-care attitude, and the pervasive mentality summed up in the words of the latest pop star:

Because you don't know us at all
We laugh when old people fall,
But what would you expect with a conscience so small?
—Sum 41

This is why I've coined the term "rappority."

The Job

You can quickly be relegated as a brownnoser if you are try-ing to exert influence at work. Your biggest challenge will be trying to distinguish your cubicle or office from that of the weed smoker with a hangover next to you. Go too slow and be a slacker, or go too fast and you're a butt kisser. It has become a full-time job just trying not to rock the boat. All too often I hear the same worn-out story: "You have to understand my situation; I'm just trying to stay afloat!" That is precisely why people don't succeed and why rappority is the answer.

The Community

The community you live in is created by a small handful of people. Most of us don't even realize that the policies and guidelines set forth in each community are the direct result of just a few people who rise up and fight. Actually, no, it's the ones who show up and speak. If you saw who was doing most of the representation for you at homeowners-association (HOA) and city-council meetings, at the school board and your state capital, you'd freak out! Being the loudest and most annoying has become the way to get anyone's attention, but rapporin can change that.

If you're like me, you've already felt the difficulty and frustration of getting people's attention, but let's take a look at a new approach specifically designed for this generation of creative young thinkers. The answer comes to us from a collaboration of three words concatenated to make a new one. When the three combine, a new ideology emerges.

Relationship + Rapport + Authority = *Rapporin!*

This new word signifies the relationship adults should have with their teenage leaders, as well as the relationship we all have with our peers. When there is a strategic process initiated within your group, in which relationships and emotional connections are first established, followed by rapport (i.e., a mutual feeling of positive flow), and then lastly by authority (i.e., service leadership with boundaries) to create an optimistic culture within the organization, people explode into their untapped potential. In the best examples of successful youth groups, communities, and professional groups, the characteristics that laid the foundation for progress were as follows:

- Love for the fellow members (emotion)
- A clear sense of *mutual* direction (connection)
- Clear-cut boundaries and rules to guide members to shared goals (protection)

Gone are the days of dictatorial and coercive authoritarians. No one responds (for long) to fear-of-loss management.

The management framework of teams is now the model for leadership on campus, in your community, and at the workplace. The artistry you create for the people you serve will be demonstrated through your ability to share their experiences. When people can reach and enjoy the critical mass of rappority, expect records to be broken by volunteer or professional efforts. Expect the attitude of service to be obvious to observers. Expect a renewed sense of purpose to permeate your meetings. And, most importantly, expect a greater awareness of citizenship to reside within the newly born leaders we continue to rely upon for tomorrow's world.

Ten Critical Leadership Seconds

Rappority is a great baseline to establish in all your interactions with people. The following is a list of one-second leadership moments in which your actions will have a dramatic effect on the outcomes you desire. Practice them and watch for them; commit them to your memory, and they will open new doors of opportunity for you.

Moment 1: The moment of unforgettable introduction. You will definitely notice how people respond to you if your introduction to them is not positive. This also applies to how you introduce others. Capture this moment, and you will live forever in the other's mind. Let this moment pass, and you will be forgotten like a piece of human junk mail.

Moment 2: A moment of astute observation. If you can be constantly aware of your surroundings and situations, you're bound to observe what others don't see. The split second in which you notice a particular unseen angle can make all the difference in how you respond and how others respond to you.

Moment 3: A moment of insightful intuition. People are always astounded by the person who seems to understand more clearly than others the complexities of life. By running scenarios through in your mind in every facet and perspective, you'll develop an uncanny sense of wise intuition. This skill can take years to fully mature, but when it is cultivated to its most awesome potential, a split second of intuition can be extraordinary.

Moment 4: A moment of penetrating wit. If you can hone your skills as a communicator, the mental dance that takes place every day between all people will allow you the rare fortune of showing off your mind. This requires your tongue to be ready as the poetic delivery system for your sculpted intellect. Practice how you'd like to say your opinion; make it a masterful ode to the lost virtue of being clever.

Moment 5: A moment of timeless humor. To give the gift of laughter to people requires a profound understanding of tragedy. You see, all humor requires crossing the boundaries of conventional thought. Those who can adeptly step back and forth over the line without injury to others will appear almost godlike and will command an unmistakable appeal. Look for the humor in all circumstances and feel closely for the line. Take some chances to inject a memorable laugh at the critical second and watch the gamble pay off big.*

*This is a critical second that must be tempered with moment 10; the two must be congruently mastered for them to be effective.

Moment 6: A moment of purest compassion. Your appreciation of this moment will be illuminated when you are the beneficiary of a compassionate heart. Unfortunately, we will all suffer from loss or weakness at various times in our lives. In these times, humans in their most vulnerable state lay bare their delicate beliefs about their own well-being. As a leader, you will have the unique insight to view these situations with a sense of shared experience. Your good deeds will surely bring you respect, for all good deeds are rewarded in due time. Your good heart can brilliantly shine for a grandiose moment that will indelibly mark those who encounter your second of purest compassion.

Moment 7: A moment of devout faith. No matter what your religion dictates in regard to doctrine and practice, all enduring faiths strengthen mankind with an ideology of hope. This moment is the easiest to fake, but age and wisdom soon reveal the scams. In this powerful second, true and total assurance in the face of mind-boggling adversity cultivates a hotbed for miracles. The trust of the just is a recurring theme throughout the myths and methods of faithful believers. When one stands before the giants of challenge and temptation and can operate as an empowered visionary, one second of convincing truthful faith will solidify the doubts of millions.

Moment 8: A moment of courageous boldness. As exemplified by the heroes of war and history, this moment is not absent of fear. What is distinct about one second of boldness is the total possession allowed for a person of conviction. When one is physically consumed with the driving force of his or her inner voice, people stop and stare. Stand courageously when others fearfully sit, and emblaze forever your memory on the hearts and minds of all who behold you.

Moment 9: A moment of selfless generosity. This moment carries with it an almost sacred exclusivity. To give in the wealth of abundance is a noble deed; to give as a sacrifice for others at your own expense is divine. Your motives must be true, and your actions must be secret; this is the highest challenge of this critical second. The shaping effect of this moment will greatly impact the receiver and will profoundly define the character of the giver. When you see this epiphany in real life, you will feel as though you are seeing something that only God himself should see.

Moment 10: A moment of perfect silence. This entire book is hinged on this miraculous second. All of eternity and only a wink reside in the fullness of this doorway. Every human effort to find the answers to life's toughest questions will be discovered in this tiny gap between infinity and the present. Seek this path and allow it to find you and tap the momentum and wisdom of all that binds us together. Be filled and empty at the same time and recognize the flow of man's existence. Quiet the distractions that handcuff your brilliance. Allow your internal guidance system to plot a trajectory of signifi-cance through your most creative and passionate endeavors, and embark upon the epic saga that defines mankind.

Getting on Track

The lost power of independent individual thought in our daily routines has created some new challenges for emerging leaders. When people are controlled by mindless mass-media distraction, your influence can easily drown in an ocean of overstimulation. Observe the interactions of people; most times, you see a sickening display of selfish inclination.

Common civility is an acquired skill, mastered by previous generations that we now marginalize with quick and easy labels. Masterful leadership has been exemplified in a stun-ning array of people in much harder and more complex times than these. The information age has given birth to a mentality that allows younger (less prudent, less wise, and less discrimi-nate) people to deem their potential mentors obsolete. Incremental differences in style, technological savvy, and age are now perceived as impenetrable compartments, not as the usual generation gap.

The building blocks of wisdom are constructed upon (1) identifying information as valid, (2) relating the information to your context, and (3) executing your decision-making influence upon your situation. This process happens in a sec-ond. Experts call this moment "media literacy," but I feel that this is a second that reaches far beyond just the media. There are unfortunately some obstacles that present themselves at the onset of this common wisdom.

Like the bullet trains in Japan, your most brilliant offerings to the world have momentum and a track in which they follow. Imagine your ideas riding on the neuropathways of your brain on tracks created by the world's perception of you and by your own perception of yourself. As you guide your ideas to those times and places in which they will have the greatest impact, you must pass through a final threshold. Through this oracle, your most significant projections will either derail or find their homes in the hearts of immortality.

Chapter Summary

Rappority is a mixture of the elements of great leadership. How do these elements fit into your leadership style?

Relationship?

Rapport?

Authority?

Of the ten critical leadership seconds, which ones have you experienced?

Give examples: _____

_____

_____

Have you ever experienced a sense of quiet assurance during a moment of silence?

Chapter Seven

The Threshold of Relevance

I don't know what your destiny will be, but one thing I know: the only ones among you who will be really happy are those who will have sought and found how to serve.

Albert Schweitzer

Of all the factors that affect a message, this is the one that can unhinge the best ideas from the best people. If your message is deemed irrelevant, you're done. Consumption of information happens in impulses; it's quick and decisive. Imagine the human mind as a matrix of ladders. On every ladder is the value assigned to a particular thought. The higher the position on the ladder, the more value is assigned. This idea was first presented in the 1970s by the foremost expert on marketing, Alan Reis.

Reis proposed that no matter how creative or expensive or clever a message is, if there is no value assigned to the information, the campaign won't be effective. So, for your message to reach its target, there must be solid confidence that what you have to say somehow benefits the listener. This is only established by finding and delivering your message through what I call the *threshold of relevance*.

In 1992, I started my first full-time position leading students. At twenty-one years old, I was hired as the youth director for an up-and-coming suburban church. The position required that I appeal to students of ages twelve through early twenties to get them to attend, and ultimately to incorporate them into the church as members and givers. The church had a growing budget and a growing population, but up until that time, the church's youth program had not been very effective. I remember meeting with a small but loyal group of students. On a good night, there would be ten to fifteen for the midweek meeting. Being young, myself, along with working on a rap album, having a dynamic reputation, and succeeding an older gentleman, gave a positive contrast to my efforts, and the kids were excited. This was the beginning of a seven-year adventure exploring new ways to impact a very discriminating audience.

My first obstacle was to turn the stale and boring idea of attending church into an alive and exciting event. Soon I found that there was a choice to be made about whom I wanted to reach. I could try to appeal to those who were already attending another church and get them to switch, or I could try to get the kids already in attendance to bring their friends from school who may have never even dreamed of coming to a church youth meeting. I chose to reach the *unchurched* bunch. This defining decision was the key to unlocking the secrets of effective leadership. The challenges were formidable. First, to reach a teen audience, I had to compete with pop culture's negative messages. Then there was the task redefining the role of church for students who wanted nothing to do with the stagnant old buildings of yesteryear's Sunday school. And, finally, I had to make the church's hierarchies buy into valuing these "troublemaker" kids. It seemed the task was going to require a perfect storm for it all to fit together.

Over the next seven years, at two different churches, I built two tremendously successful youth programs centered on meeting students in the threshold of relevance. Hundreds of youth attended and participated in what is still considered some of the most effective youth ministry in the history of those churches. I didn't stop with just attendance; I also launched a positive-impact music festival and youth event that stands as a pinnacle of cross-denominational unity. Let me clarify. I didn't get *involved* with an organization to help plan and promote the event. I mortgaged my house to raise the hundred thousand dollars it took to rent out all three of Arizona's top water parks.

We wanted to create a unique experience for all of the attendants, so we secured the parks all night. This was a task that no one else had done before or since. From the humble beginnings of six hundred kids, over the next five consecutive years our ministry grew to drawing over five thousand in our final two years, and our event (The Rage) was a legendary success. From The Rage Youth Event, I collaborated with a record company to coproduce young talent, and from this emerged four compilation CDs. These projects helped some blossoming talent get record deals. To promote the event throughout the year, I held concerts with some of the biggest names in Christian music. These concerts gave me backstage exclusivity and the inside track to influencing youth. So I launched a radio show called exactly that, *The Inside Track*. The radio show became the only teen talk show in Arizona. We gave students a voice to share their views on the world around them. We didn't preach to them, and in that vein we uncovered a great secret. When presented with relevant information and the opportunity and empowerment to get involved, students overwhelmingly excel.

Some people will always expect a replication of tactics to duplicate previous results. I realize that the things I did to get the attention of my target audience will not necessarily work for others. On Hip-Hop Night, we had a break-dancing contest and a live DJ. On X Night, we paid homage to extreme games, and we brought Trevor Myer, a four-time X-Games champion BMX freestyler, for an exhibition to illustrate the point.

Our students competed for the Christian radio station against other secular stations in a lip-synching contest and won! They secured for the station the use of four billboards around town and received citywide recognition.

Our youth group exploded to over 150 regular attendees on a small night and over 200 on a big night—at a church that only boasted 250 adult members! We called our place "The Zone." Now, I want to remind you that an exclusive bunch of leaders at big megachurches will always tout the secrets to building an appealing environment, but I'm not trying to compete with the impossible. I'm saying that in small communities, in realistic-size schools and groups, one second in the threshold of relevance will change the outcome of all your efforts.

The next challenge was money. Our own internal fundraising was responsible for buying the church van and the audiovisual system for the building, as well as for paying for computers, curricula, promotion, special-speaker fees, music, and thousands of dollars for special charity projects. The students paid for it all! One second in the threshold of relevance can yield the highest financial rewards.

The truth behind the challenge is that there *is* money available to pay for all the positive initiatives we want; there just isn't the *vision* or the *value* placed on those ideas we *say* are important to us. You see that advertisers will spend millions of dollars on the gamble that their product will succeed, but we have a hard time raising a few hundred bucks to launch our ideas. The grassroots movement it takes to get people involved doesn't start with a huge budget; it starts with a huge *belief.* Deliver that belief through the threshold of relevance and watch it explode.

Evolving in the Threshold

Over the last fifteen years, I have worked with hundreds of groups that are focused on youth. It has been my privilege and joy to be involved with every one of them. There is, however, one particular organization that has emblazoned its impact upon my heart and captured the passion of teenagers around the world, and it is lead by a man in his eighties. HOBY stands for Hugh O'Brian Youth Leadership. Hugh O'Brian is the Yoda of youth development! This former television and movie star has beautifully defined the idea that it takes young people to change young people. His story is fascinating.

In 1958, thirty-three-year-old Hugh O'Brian was at the top of his game. With striking good looks, this leading-man actor had a regular television role as the famous Western hero/lawman Wyatt Earp. Now, this was before cable television, but millions tuned in every week, and, with only two or three channels, everyone knew who Hugh was. To give you a modern example, Hugh was the Brad Pitt or Tom Cruise of his day. On a trip to Africa, Hugh met the legendary humanitarian Albert Schweitzer.

Albert Schweitzer was a medical doctor, philosopher, and theologian who dedicated his life and profession to his reverence-for-life ideology. His core beliefs sprang from his idea that mankind was decaying from its loss of love for life. Through thought and a commitment to kindness, Schweitzer proposed a life of awareness, individuality, and charity for all the earth's inhabitants. He was recognized for his humanitarian work in Africa, and he died in 1965 in Lambarene (French Equatorial Africa).

Hugh, from this life-changing experience, made a radical turn in his life and started helping students develop the integral skill of critical thinking. He did this by founding summer conferences aimed at developing leadership skills in high school sophomores. Hugh's visionary intuition ushered a message of inspired motivated minds to students who were desperately confused about their place in the world.

Taking up the job of motivating people commonly thought to be lazy and unambitious was no small task. The hardest part must have been that Hugh's message had to compete with the defining messages of pop culture. His voice had to be poignant enough to make sense to people who didn't always want to hear positive and empowering advice. Hugh skillfully parlayed his celebrity status into timeless words of inspiration and direction. Thousands of students were able to find themselves and a path to success in a complicated world. But that was only the beginning of his remarkable story.

The real high point of this incredible man's legacy is that it has yet to climax. Hugh is now eighty years old. He is overseeing leadership seminars in fifty states and hosting one of the most prestigious world conferences, held every year in Washington, D.C. Politicians, movie stars, musicians, and leaders of the corporate world, as well as 335,000 HOBY ambassadors, recognize Hugh's forty-six years of service as an enduring living legend of youth development. The most amazing and awe-inspiring aspect of this story is how Hugh has continued to evolve into the new century. He has enlisted an army of thousands of volunteers who keep the momentum and message firmly residing within the threshold of relevance. Hugh isn't recognized in public the way he once was. He isn't hounded for autographs or stalked by paparazzi. No one really cares who he's dating or how much weight he's lost or gained. He is, however, recognized by some of the world's most influential leaders as the foremost authority on creating multiple generations of leaders. I believe time will reveal that Hugh's contribution has had a more substantial impact than any of today's twenty-million-dollar pop culture icons.

The Power of Your Voice

So now you're excited about your group or school or organization, but how do you find the threshold of relevance?

How do you know if you're there? Maybe you've experienced exactly what I'm talking about, a time in your life when you felt everyone was listening, responding, and just naturally following your leadership. Over time, maybe that has

> The strategy you want to enlist is to align yourself within the flow of actions and thoughts that relate to people's lives.

gotten harder. Maybe you find yourself repeating excuses aimed at convincing yourself that the people you work with are different. Maybe you think you're too young to start exerting your influence on others.

The fact is that the threshold of relevance is an evolving flow. You must constantly find ways to get into that flow. So don't think in terms of tactics and strategies, because those will change over time. Think of your efforts in terms of *alignment.* The strategy you want to enlist is aligning yourself within the flow of actions and thoughts that relate to people's lives. People have to see you in the light of that which *they* value. That means you have to relate to them in terms of bringing value to their situation. Take a look at the following list. You must align yourself within the beliefs of your audience.

1. Your audience needs to believe that you are a credible source of information.

2. Your audience needs to believe that you are willing to sacrifice personally.

3. Your audience needs to believe that you are sharing their experiences with them.

4. Your audience needs to believe that you have practical answers and solutions to the problems they face.

5. Your audience needs to believe that you are informed and empowered with the latest, most relevant information.

6. Your audience needs to believe that you are secure in your ability to work with other dynamic leaders.

I've deliberately chosen the word "audience" to describe the people around you every day. They are the ones who want to experience something special from their leaders. Your stage is set every time you interact with them. This is also why I believe so strongly in public speaking as a top priority for every leader. I'll talk more about that later, but to begin the idea, I simply want to originate the basic concept of articulation.

Watch the interactions people have each day. If you look closely, you'll see an awkward dance of miscommunication at every turn. People walk around lost when signs telling them exactly where they are stare them in the face. In a confused manner, they wander through their daily routines hoping someone will tell them what to do. It often seems we have no original thoughts at all. This is why it is so crucial that more of us stand up and communicate. Talk! Instead of grunting our intentions to other cave dwellers or thumbing our text-message abbreviations through cyberspace, we need to learn how to speak our intentions in full, easy-to-understand sentences. Articulation is a skill the information age has deadened in us. We are constantly hearing someone else's persuasive message—so much so that we have inadvertently taught ourselves to act upon the intentions of others. As a critical thinker, turn the tables and try the sound of your own voice on for size.

The Best Speakers Are Expert Listeners

Before you start looking for opportunities to speak publicly, it's my recommendation that you take a few opportunities to listen. The art of active listening is by far the most important leadership skill you'll ever need. When interacting with people, it is crucial that you establish an underlying trust by projecting your open mind into the dynamic of conversation. Here are a few suggestions that can be used in critical seconds that will develop your listening skills.

Engagement. Look at the person who is talking to you. Make eye contact and raise your eyebrows. Nod your head up and down in affirmation. Let your face show expressions that correctly exhibit the appropriate emotional response (e.g., sadness for bad news, excitement for good news, interest in the information being shared, just not a blank stare).

Repeat, then respond. When someone is trying to communicate with you, sometimes those attempts can be derailed by misunderstandings. One way to avoid silly arguments is to be sure you are hearing the information correctly. Take the time to let the talker finish. Then, before you get all riled up, repeat what you believe you are being told back to the talker and ask if you are hearing correctly. Many times, talkers may amend what they are saying in order to further the conversation, and they may also realize where they themselves need to adjust.

Respond immediately. Once you've allowed someone to talk to you and you understand the person correctly, take action immediately to show her that you've heard. Even if all you can do is validate her feelings by telling her that what she said is important, do it. You can also respond immediately by saying, "I'm going to approach these concerns head on, and I appreciate your input" or "Let's discuss an action plan to come up with some solutions." You may even respond by simply continuing to listen. You may say, "You've said this much; now let me hear how I should respond."

Project Your Positive Passions

In every group of people, you'll run across the same dynamics when tasks and agendas must be carried out. There will always be those who take it upon themselves to remind everyone why the group must adopt a negative viewpoint. In the spirit of "venting" or needing to get their feelings "out in the open," these naysayers are self-appointed group therapists who, under the guise of "openness," get everyone sidetracked from the really important stuff. Don't let this energy take hold of your leadership. One second of negativity can be all it takes to derail your best efforts. Muster all of your most positive and optimistic perspectives and inject them into your conversations. It's not nearly as hard as you may think to find the bright side of every situation.

If you always look for the best in people and opportunities, you'll start to see that the best people and opportunities will start to look for you. In this skeptical age, the

> If you always look for the best in people and opportunities, you'll start to see that the best opportunities and people will start to look for you.

world is starving for something authentic. People crave the truth they feel in songs and poems, scriptures and prayers. In the depths of your heart lies a dream that only you can conjure. Placed there by destiny, it will only awaken when you summon the courage to look deeply within and breathe life into this dormant gift. When you get in touch with your dream, your purpose, you'll be compelled by an inspiration that people are dying to experience. It's inarguable, and it's so empowering that your weaknesses and shortcomings will fade from focus.

Commit yourself to learning how to unleash your inner sense of purpose in truth and sincerity. One second of projecting your positive passions is enough to create a whole new atmosphere of hope and excitement. Change is born of these seeds, and the hearts of men are captured in single seconds of passionate creativity.

Find a Creative Language

One of the most effective strategies enlisted by marketing gurus is utilizing all manner of art and language to get their point across. This is not their exclusive privilege. We, too, should all look for ways to enhance our effective communication in a second of creativity. There is no underlying rule that prevents us from finding the best and most creative way to be heard. I wrote earlier about my rap music experience. I have been lucky enough to live through an era that said this new music (hip-hop) would never last. Like the generation before me that saw rock and roll emerge, I will explain to my grandchildren the evolution of a music genre. Before pop music had influence, there was classical music; before classical music, there was poetry; before poetry, there was drama; and before drama, there was ceremony and dance.

Thousands of years of human experience have paved the way for us to creatively share with others. All manner of art, sculpture, and song have been used to lead people through new endeavors. Why have we continued to let modern society choke the creativity out of our ideas? We need innovative young leaders to step forward in these dark ages of individuality and shine the light of their brilliance on enslaved consumer masses. Who said we could not use poetry to influence people anymore? Why not use dramatic skits to share a sentiment or lesson? Why is quoting the great philosophers and history's superstars considered "being a nerd"? Why is there such tremendous fear attached to allowing your own voice to be heard?

When people ask me if I think the young people of today are getting harder to reach, or if they are in worse spiritual condition, I am always torn between the frustration with how hardheaded so many students are and the legendary creativity I see in the young people of the twenty-first century. I am always most impressed with the students who have found an expression that distinguishes them in this culture of white noise. It *is* possible to discover a new way of seeing things, *your* way. This is the challenge of every individual that has the ability to ponder issues beyond the basic needs of survival. At the time of this writing, the world is focused on the disastrous tsunami that ravaged Southeast Asia. Millions of people are wondering at this moment where their next meal is coming from. Here in the United States, we have been given the greatest gift, in that we have more time than most of the world to think of ways to create a better life.

So it's my charge to a generation of young brilliant dreamers to avail yourself of this wonderful opportunity. Take one second to think, find the artistry inside yourself, and speak to the world in your most beautiful voice of individuality. Commit yourself to becoming great with skills that only you possess. Bend your ear toward the connections you've been blessed to belong to and hear the order and innate wisdom that resides in that resonance.

Chapter Summary

What is the threshold of relevance?

Do you feel you have a vision you would like to see to fruition?

    Write it out: _____

_____

_____

_____

When you are in leadership, you will always have to be aware of your audience. Do you know who *your* audience is?

The best leaders are great listeners; give some examples of when you can practice the art of listening.

_____

_____

How will you inject positive energy into your conversations?

Do you feel that it's possible to turn a negative conversation into a positive one?

Chapter Eight

The Power of Presence

A truly rich man is one whose children run into his arms when his hands are empty.

Author unknown

When seeking the voice of clarity and authenticity, you will surely hear the voices that live within your subconscious mind. Some of these voices can be ugly and negative; they are the voices of failure and defeat, and they are the unfortunate remains of dysfunction and the mistakes we all make in our journey through life. Part of your evolution as a brilliant young leader will be tied to your ability to abandon these lethal examples that take joy in your demise. You will also hear the voices of encouragement and strength whispering inspiration. Over the course of your life, you will have teachers and mentors who help you find your voice. Your voice is the quiet, confident, and dignified motivation that leads to greatness and success. These teachers will speak words of truth and wisdom to you, and their life and presence will remain with you through their actions and guidance. When you identify these teachers, embrace their contributions to your story. Grant them the respect they deserve by becoming pliable to their instruction. In time, you will notice that the lessons they have given you will reappear again and again, and as with mathematics, the solutions remain the same. The following passages are some of the dearest and most candid ideas I can share from my own life. The voice I hear every day in my presentations to students all over the country and to my own kids comes from the presence of my father, David Quan.

David Quan was a first-generation Chinese American. My grandparents came from China, and my father was born here in the United States. Growing up in the Southwest United

States, the Quans were part of a small but growing community of Asians in Phoenix, Arizona. My grandparents did what many Chinese Americans did to survive; they opened a restaurant. Even as a young boy, my father was expected to work tirelessly all day in the restaurant. In our Chinese heritage, it's common for multiple generations to carry on a family business. It's a tight-knit and exclusive culture of Chinese only. As a young man, my father was constantly reminded that he was to speak Chinese and that when the time was right, the family would travel back to China to arrange a marriage for him to a "good Chinese girl."

When my dad was a young adult, he found that the late sixties was a turbulent and exciting time to be in America. Being one of only a few Asians in his high school, young David soon discovered the joy of rock music and Harley Davidsons. Now, I know you're not used to seeing Chinese people on Harleys, but my dad was the exception. David embraced his American culture and decided he would not need to go back to China to find a wife (good thing for me). While cruising Central Avenue in Phoenix in 1970, my dad met my mom at Jack in the Box. This was the beginning of a new chapter for the Quans. At the ripe old age of twenty, my father married my mother, and they started a family with me. This young couple was ill prepared for marriage, much less a child, and sadly the marriage only lasted a year. Then, at only twenty-one, David was divorced and had a child; he had some serious choices to make. He took an entry-level job at the telephone company and applied some of his traditional Chinese work ethic. For seven years, my father worked his way into management at the telephone company and began dreaming of starting his own business.

During this time, David met and fell in love with a wonderful new woman named Peg, and they married and also began having children. They were married for twenty-three years, until the day my father died. Peg and David bought a modest home in Central Phoenix and founded their family in strong Christian faith. First came David Junior, then Ann Marie, and then Jason and Joshua. The Quan household was filled with love and devotion, and they wanted to give that love to others who were in need. This prompted them to adopt Nghia (pronounced "Nia") and Thanh (pronounced "Ton," like Tom), two Amerasian children from Vietnam. After twenty years of marriage, there was an unexpected surprise, and at nearly age forty, Peg gave birth to Kelli. This huge family inspired my father to give up one of his joys, riding Harleys.

Now, with all of these kids, you would think my dad was an expert with a switch! But to tell you the truth, He never spanked me. Being forced to grow up fast, my dad became very reserved and quiet. Though I know he loved us, I can only recall a handful of times he ever said the words, "I love you." Now, I don't want you to think he was boring and stuffy; he wasn't. In fact, he grew his hair into a shoulder-length ponytail. He also played a mean rock guitar. He started his own company based in technology and broke all the common stereotypes ingrained in his family. In a beautiful display of self-sacrifice, my dad harnessed all the passion he felt for adventure and individuality and channeled that energy into his business. He worked ruthlessly long days and scratched his success out of stone. Many times he would work to utter exhaustion, sleep on a couch at his office, wake up, and resume working again. His words were few, and you could still detect the hint of a respectful Chinese bow when he was introduced.

Those who knew my father would have characterized him as a witty but quiet man who was honest and generous, who loved his children, and whose faith spoke volumes without ever saying a word. My father's dreams lay totally wrapped in his work and family, and only on rare occasions would he admit he missed the joy of riding a Harley Davidson. The Quan household was a model for devoted families. Service and volunteer work were interwoven into the fabric of our routines. Some of the work became almost second nature and as regular as any normal family function. Working with the homeless and destitute in the inner city was just part of our everyday normalcy. Every Christmas and Thanksgiving, our family immersed itself into the spirit of giving and volunteering. As the family matured and the business grew profitable, my father's underlying dream was slowly rising to the surface. In private moments he would tell me that he'd love to ride again.

The day arrived in September 1998 when my father called to tell me that he'd finally done it; he simply stated, "I got my Harley." That very day, I went to his business. As I Arrived at the custom-built commercial building in Tempe, my dad walked me over to a small storage garage. He opened a roll-up door, and there in this small but clean area he revealed the coolest motorcycle I've ever seen. Black leather and chrome mixed with the distinctive Harley Davidson rumble, and I could see why he was so in love. He asked me if I wanted to go to lunch on the bike, and I jumped at the chance. I got on the backseat, and as I was giddy as a schoolgirl, my dad had to tell me to take my hands off his waist and hold the back bar. I'll never forget those moments of pride and freedom as we sped down Southern Avenue to lunch that day. I was the only child who got to ride the Harley with him.

September 26, 1998, was the day that forced me to stop and look deeply at the meaning behind the voices we take for granted so often. I came home from a day of shopping and saw that I had a message on my answering machine. I pressed the button and heard the sound of my stepmother's voice.

"Leon, your father was in a serious motorcycle accident today, and we need you to call Scottsdale Memorial Hospital."

I picked up the phone and dialed. A woman answered the phone, and I asked to speak with David Quan. The woman's voice stuttered, and she said, "You'll have to speak with his wife." The phone was shuffled, and Peg answered. "Leon, your dad was in a serious motorcycle accident today...and he died."

Remembering those devastating moments still chokes me up. It's hard even now, years later, to explain the all-consuming loneliness of losing a parent. For those of you who have been through the grieving process, I'm sure you have an idea. For those of you who haven't, I wouldn't wish it on my worst enemy. I can admit it now; I wasn't ready for that kind of emotional process. The candid reality is that I fell apart on the inside and on the outside. In one grief-stricken moment, I vomited from the stress and gut-wrenching turmoil. One memory that has haunted me is the image of my sibling's tears creating the artwork of grief on the tile floor of my parents family room as we huddled together to comfort one another the first time we came together after my father's death. During the funeral, I remember my younger brother Jason (who has a reputation for being gregarious and fun loving) doubling over as he wept for our father. That time in my life is still a blur when I try to recall certain facts. I spoke to hundreds of people, and yet I can't recall any of those conversations. Not until nearly a year later did I have any clarity on what this experience meant to me. The conclusions I arrived at concerning who I am and what my life is supposed to mean mark me to this day. I learned some valuable lessons in that period following my father's death. I would like to share some of those valuable insights with you.

At fifteen years old, every boy passes through the adolescent gauntlet that allows him to question the authority of his father. I was no different. After supper, the dinner table was a chore left to the kids in our household. Mom made it, and we had to clean it up. Looking back now, it was a pretty equitable arrangement. For whatever reason, this particular night found me in a testy mood, and I defiantly walked away from the table and left the chores to my little brothers and sisters. My stepmother immediately requested that I assist in this regular family endeavor. For my first act of rebellion, I thought I'd be original and mouth off a little. Again, I see a little more clearly now, but at fifteen, I was in uncharted waters. Teenage defiance has a system that I've identified, and it has predictable steps; I'm sure you'll be familiar with them. First, I furrowed my eyebrows. Then I started spitting through my consonant sounds: *ca, waa, da, pa*! Then I began asking in a whiny SpongeBob SquarePants voice, "What if I don't want to?" My father was calm, but I saw a question on his face as one of his eyebrows raised. He slowly rose from the table and made his way toward the back door. "Leon, why don't you step out back with me for a moment?" Being an older brother, I could tell from the admiration in the younger ones that I'd better put on an entertaining show. I sauntered toward the door and winked confidently at my little disciples. They looked at each other: *this is gonna be good!*

My father was a very stoic and unemotional man; he was known more for his silence than for the words he spoke, and I read that as weakness. It sort of startled me when he began to speak. He began to review how my attitude had had an effect on the others in the house. As he recounted the offenses, I heard his tone begin to change, and more emphasis was placed at the end of each statement. This was not the David Quan I was used to. His lecture quickly intensified, as I'm sure he noticed the belittling roll of my eyes—not the smartest thing I've ever done. My father stood directly in front of me and in an uncharacteristic style balled both of his hands into fists. He screamed a final challenge at me and then pushed/punched me right in the chest. "If you think you're so *bad*, Leon, go ahead and take your best shot!"

May the validity of this book rest in this one teachable moment.

I didn't know what to do. I glanced back at the windowed rear door to see six sets of sibling eyes anxiously awaiting the next few moments. (I think they were placing bets.)

Turning back to face my father, I deduced quickly that I was at a crossroads. I could scream a challenge back at him and assume the "crane stance" (visions of Ralph Macchio fleet quickly in real life). The other choice was to cower and submit to his authority. When I looked inside myself to summon the courage I'd need to make this a respectable fight, the only emotion present was fear and weakness placed on full display through huge uncontrollable tears.

Without any dignity remaining to defend myself, I was left to sob out threats about "calling Child Protective Services to report a child abuser." This, of course, got me a good laugh from the peanut gallery. "Shut up!" I whined. My father, sensing that my defiance was broken, took the next few moments to center himself. I turned away, broken and humiliated, hunched over through my hyperventilating heaves. Then, in a stunning example of paternal wisdom, David Quan arrived at himself and became Daddy again. He moved beside me and placed his arm around my shoulders in an encouraging embrace. Without any hesitation, this regularly unaffectionate man began telling me how much I meant to him. He told me I was smart and valuable and that he loved me. He met my brokenness and insecurity with strength and showed me the responsibility of having the name Quan. He took the opportunity to reach me by asking questions and letting me openly communicate with him. He wasn't condescending or dismissive, and he talked more openly than I'd ever seen before. In full view of his children, my father unabashedly modeled a devotion to me that I now look back at and pinpoint. That conversation and those critical moments are some of the single most defining experiences of my life. Being a father now, I realize he was probably never that mad at all, just afraid I wouldn't be clear about what is most important in life. Thanks again, Dad.

These memories came crashing down on me as we planned my father's funeral. Although my family had not embraced traditional Chinese culture in our home, there were a few traditions from our heritage that we adopted. It's customary to offer a gift to those who attend a Chinese funeral—a small piece of candy wrapped together with a coin. The candy is for sweetness to soothe the pain of grief, and the coin represents good fortune. We began to calculate the scope of the funeral and prepare these little tokens accordingly. In that reflective time, our family anticipated that 100 to 150 people would attend the funeral. How many people would come to the funeral of this quiet Chinese business owner? My father was a shy and relatively obscure man, but he was well loved by the people who knew him. I can still visualize sitting in the front row of our home church and staring at the mementos of my dad's life, a dark green casket surrounded with pictures, flowers, and the little-known knickknacks that identified David Quan—cowboy boots, guitars, and motorcycles. Though my grief was blinding during that ceremony, I can still recall being moved by the outpouring of support from the people who knew and loved my father—all one thousand of them! That's right; a thousand people attended the funeral. All of them had a story, too! You see, we thought our family were the only people who knew what a great man David Quan was. It became glaringly clear that my quiet father had for many years secretly cultivated a great love for his community and business and for those less fortunate. They greeted us warmly and told us of the many times David Quan had lent them money, had brought them food, or had fixed their car. What a profound impression was left on us through my father's final lesson.

David Quan had learned something in his life that was not tied to charisma or public displays of piety. He had lived on a deeper, more essential level and had captured what I call "the power of presence." He had found the truth of life in himself and had allowed it to emerge in his daily interactions with people. He had given himself over to being moved by his heart for those around him, and as a habit he drew upon this idea to arrive at himself when he acted. He was never coerced into charity or manipulated into service. My father's actions could not have been measured while he was alive, and his personality never even hinted that his ego was gratified by his generosity. I have a very different personality than my father did, but as a father now myself, and as a more extraverted person, the lesson is sealed deep inside my mind. You don't have to be the loudest or tallest or best looking to make a substantial impact on the world around you. You don't have to have a ton of money or an Ivy League education to gain the gritty and visceral authenticity that comes from reaching people. But you *do* have to come to grips with the innate wisdom that defines you. You must connect with the purpose your life has been endowed with. You, too, can arrive at yourself in every critical moment and act with a stunning display of the gift we all have but shamefully neglect: the ability to care.

Chapter Summary

Who in your life has established a presence that you gain inspiration from?

Whose life have you established a presence within?

What truth have you found in your life that helps you arrive at yourself and exemplify presence?

Can you recall a time when in a critical second you captured the power of presence?

What are some important times you would like to be more present for?

    Give examples: _____

_____

_____

Chapter Nine

The Seven Critical Seconds of Excellence

To resist the frigidity of old age, one must combine the body, the mind, and the heart. And to keep these in parallel vigor, one must exercise, study, and love.

Alan Bleasdale

In order to make my presentations, engagement agreements, or even this book practical as well inspirational, it's important to recognize those split seconds that aren't so exciting at first glance. These are the portals of execution. They are the brutally honest and penetrating moments that everyone must face. They fly in the face of much of the motivational material we are saturated with daily. To some, they may even be deemed offensive, but I am willing to take that chance in hopes that you will see the full spectrum of what's at stake. These moments aren't fun or popular. These moments separate the strong from the weak. They redirect your focus and sharpen the effectiveness of your efforts. You will be amazed at the way certain aspects of success will seem to fall into your lap—a new contact, a huge opportunity, or maybe just the right answer at the right time. As the old saying goes, "Luck is the intersection of skill and preparation." What seems like a miracle breakthrough is really just the following seconds revealing their value in practical ways.

1. **The second in which work ethic is conceived.** I'm always amazed at how eager we are to adopt the adage "work smarter not harder." Though efficiency is an important aspect to our efforts, we are constantly focused on sellable ideas like "avoiding burnout" or "pacing ourselves." Here's what you really need to hear, and this is probably one of the only places you'll hear it: *You must work extremely hard until you succeed.* Tenacity is a dying character trait. The outcomes of your life will be directly tied

to your long hours, lack of sleep, continuous improvement, and concerted effort. Show me a failed endeavor, and I will show you a lack of work ethic in one critical part of the project. The forty-hour workweek and the eight-hour workday are humane guidelines for employers, but our internal time clock should dictate another standard for our efforts. It reads, "We'll rest when the work is done."

2. **The second in which charisma is adopted.** No more touchy-feely excuses allowing mediocrity to infect our concept of ourselves. You do not have to be born with all the benefits of height, weight, beauty, money, personality, or intelligence, but doggone it, people *have* to like you! Charisma is not outgunning everyone else when it comes to interpersonal relationships. It's finding the unique qualities that make you special and allowing those qualities to benefit those around you. Everyone has a little something that no one else has. Our genetic code guarantees it. Search for your little something, be obsessed with identifying it, and you'll discover your own charisma. When you develop an approachable magnetism, you'll experience the necessary framework for success. Henry Kissinger is best known for his dry and characteristically bland disposition; however, his best work has been achieved as a U.S. diplomat by which he has established a globally respected reputation. He has been called upon by seven American presidents over

forty years to aid in the most sensitive foreign-affairs matters. Kissinger's charisma is his deliberate ability to set his audience at ease with his unassuming and nonchalant personality.

3. **The second in which you become terrified of failure.** Can you imagine what would happen if the lions of the Serengeti Plain were to teach their cubs that they could go through life and never hunt down a gazelle? They could explain to all the neighboring predators that little Simba is not as fast as the prey and that he should just pretend he caught it, and everyone should applaud the effort when he mimes eating his kill. If this were a plausible scenario in nature, we would surmise quickly that the little lion would soon starve to death. We humans are caught in the rat's maze of our own higher thinking. Our tendency is to rationalize away the healthy fears that motivate us all, because they aren't pleasurable. We coddle our young and reinforce the idea that just making an effort is success. If we continue to cushion the rough edges of reality, we are destined to live in a world where everyone is slapping each other on the back for high-jumping over the limbo bar. "There's nothing to fear but fear itself" That's bull! Fear failure and disgrace and humiliation; fear mediocrity and underperformance; fear limiting behaviors and associations; and most of all, fear excuses and being too easy on yourself.

4. **The second in which you get strategically organized.** Your best-laid plans will only work if you give them a playing field to thrive on. The chasm between the plans that succeed and the plans that fail can be measured by the distance between the inspired idea and the skillful implementation. In my early days of youth work, I was always throwing out ideas and rarely following them through. I was always excited to start a new project, but I always hated the busywork required to see the dream through to fruition. When you take the organization of the project and make it the most deliberate and strategic component, you'll see where the sizzle of an idea really is. Get enthused about the organization and planning stages. You can't overplan. Don't let people tell you that their project requires spontaneity and improvisation, or that the pieces will just come together. That is a sure sign that the project will fail.

5. **The second in which you raise one aspect of your performance to an art form.** Naturally talented people have a well-rounded mix of skill sets. They seem to flow in and out of various accomplishments as though they were born with God's hand upon them. Then there are the rest of us. We all have the ability to work our functional routines. For some, it seems that mere survival is the goal. But for people who want their game to rise to the next level, they must carve a masterpiece from one of their abilities. This development should result in more than an

easy-to-copy skill; it should be the trademark of your work. Hours of practice and thought will result in the signature of excellence. What is your claim to fame? Why are your fingerprints so recognizable? Search out the difference in you and call it forward. Take one aspect of your personality and make it so poignant that people will feel special when they encounter it.

6. **The second in which your stretch goal isn't a stretch.** In all of your efforts, the most gratifying time you'll ever encounter is when everything that you've hoped for becomes a reality. Goal setting is a standard practice for everyone; however, goal attainment is where many get a little fuzzy.

> You can't over do success; it may be a virtue to mercifully dominate a lesser team in sports (I'll grant that fact to little league baseball), but in the game of life run your victories as high as you can!

Oftentimes, goal redefinition substitutes for 100 percent achievement. So, to avoid failing, we set increments for our goals. Way out in the land of "that outcome would be a miracle" is the place where legends live. Sometimes you have to overachieve to truly make your point. When you've already satisfied everyone else, finishing with the same vitality you started with and achieving 120 percent of your goal is the part of the project you do for yourself. You can't overdo success. It may be a virtue to mercifully dominate a lesser team in sports

(I'll grant that fact to Little League baseball), but in the game of life, run your victories as high as you can. Don't stop needlessly to rest when you've barely accomplished the goal. You may only appreciate your achievements when you are undeniably, categorically, unabashedly, unapologetically, undisputedly the best at what you do.

7. **The second in which you duplicate your effective habits.** This is the critical second of excellence that happens the moment you're able to reproduce greatness in others. Identifying the potential in other people and helping them release their best talents is a skill very few master. Your true test will be whether you can draw forth the best potential from those who have greater skill than you do. Will your ego be able to endure seeing someone else promoted? Fall in love with the development of others and make their success your goal. Adopt an attitude that relies on your family or community or colleagues. Make yourself subject to the greatness of others you have helped, and feel the momentum of excellence within your own greatness.

> Make yourself subject to the greatness of others that you have helped and feel the momentum of excellence within your own greatness.

My critics will probably say that I'm oversimplifying with the "one-second" theme. They'll say that real-life situations take more than one second, but I disagree. In the next few passages, I'd like to reveal some real-life dynamics that can be engineered in the blink of an eye. View these ideas as split-second pathways into a greater perspective. Just like a persistent child, keep observing these moments as opportunities to get something. They may not always bear out in your behalf, but you'll see quick glimpses of a favorable dynamic that is bound to benefit you. In short, try to imagine these moments as lottery tickets. If I gave you one, you'd say thanks, but your hopes wouldn't be too high. If I gave you thousands, you'd realize that the odds were in your favor to win. When you first begin your journey into leadership, you will not be successful every time you make an attempt. However, if you seek out these moments, identify them, and implement them into your skill sets, *look out*!

One-Second Dynamics

Positive conversation. Segue sentences can be delivered in only a second and can be effective tools for swinging a conversation in a different direction. One of the ways people cope with stress is to vent it to whoever will listen. When people start this airing of their frustration, fear, and hopelessness, it's almost a sacrilege to take their negativity away from them. To correct them or tell them that they are bringing you down seems to inflame them even more. Are you thinking of someone specific right now? Have you ever been cornered by a person who wears a perpetual frown and can never utter a syllable of good news? These people will always be with us; it's human nature to seek support and validation from others we care about. If you really need to vent your problems, do it when you're by yourself, and vent them to your higher purpose.

Your purpose will always bring you strength and encouragement. You see, the problem is that this conversational disease is contagious! Without even knowing it, you can catch an STD! That's right, a "sour-talk disease." This can lead to a nasty case of SFD, or "sour-face disease," and of course then there is the really ugly (and potentially fatal) strain of SLD, or "sour-life disease." A great way to prevent this from taking over any conversation is to use a one-second conversational prefix. Before you start to talk, just say, "I need to say something positive right now," and then continue speaking. If you are in the middle of a meeting that isn't productive due to negative attitudes, use a segue sentence to redirect the flow: "How can we be focused on a positive solution?" or "I heard someone say something that really inspired me once, and it was this…." Here are a few segue sentences that you can commit to memory. Make them adapt to your particular situation.

- ❑ "I want to be part of an exciting and empowering project."
- ❑ "I think there is a solution that we can discover together."
- ❑ "I can hear that there are some passionate people here; how can we tap that passion for some solutions?"
- ❑ "I've heard the bad news; what's the good news?"
- ❑ "I'm involved because I'm inspired; what inspires you?"

These simple sentences shouldn't be said with sarcasm in your voice. They should be little reminders that the direction any conversation takes is controlled by the people talking. The outcomes that arise from meetings, friendships, or associations are directly related to the positive attitudes of the people involved. Try to make up some of your own segue sentences and watch how people will regard you as a source of positive and proactive energy within any relationship.

Positive group interaction. The way people perceive you is reality to them. If you are an intelligent and ambitious individual, yet people see you acting lazy and unenthused, then no matter

> **The fact remains, no one follows the ignorant.**

what you *say* about yourself, to them you are a louse! Controlling every critical second of your life will prevent others from ever misperceiving your true intentions. In groups, watch the dynamic when people perceive you for just one second in the following terms:

- ❑ **One second of intelligence.** It seems to have become a sin to be recognized as an intelligent human being. The mediocre and the stupid have risen to rock-star status when it comes to the young. The fact remains, though, that no one follows the ignorant. Take one second and allow your clever and intelligent personality to be seen. Observe the subtle ways people will gravitate to you for the gift of your knowledge and advice.

❑ **One second of eloquence.** Mastering language is fundamental to excellent leadership. To be concise and clear with your vocabulary will affect the poignancy of your skills. Practice advancing your word usage and conversational syntax. Be the person who always knows what to say, and people will listen.

❑ **One second of relevance.** In the information age, being uninformed is an unforgivable leadership faux pas. Take strides toward filling up on fresh information. Read some source of daily news and be familiar with subjects that directly relate to your community. Make your words ooze with value by imparting credible knowledge that helps those listening. Understand what you are talking about before commenting. Show prudence by controlling your urge to judge without all the information.

If you begin to raise these dynamics as golden rules within your leadership style, you'll see some of the most miraculous moments occur before your eyes. I know some of these sound simple, but why aren't more people using these guidelines? The answer is even simpler: laziness. Enact the process of committing yourself to these situations and dynamics and identify in your circles how well others respond to you.

Chapter Summary

Which of the seven seconds of excellence would be the most immediate challenge for you? Why?

Do you feel that segue sentences would turn negative conversations into positive ones?

Give examples of some segue sentences you'll use: _____

_____

_____

_____

Controlling the way others perceive you will allow your leadership to flourish. Give some ways intelligence, relevance, and eloquence will assist you.

_____

_____

_____

Chapter Ten

One-Second Lessons
for Young Leaders

You couldn't get hold of the things you'd done and turn them right again. Such a power might be given to the gods, but it was not given to women and men, and that was probably a good thing. Had it been otherwise, people would probably die of old age still trying to rewrite their teens.

Stephen King

This chapter has been dedicated to the thousands of students who have heard my presentations and then written me letters or sent postcards. To occupy one second of your life honors me greatly and is my one of my greatest joys.

Being young in the new millennium is tougher than most people think. I know every old-timer is thinking to himself, "If they only knew how tough I had it!" but hands down, being a student today is the hardest it's ever been. The following story is a modern-day parable that explicitly details some of the critical seconds that make up a teenager's identity. It is a true story. The idea behind sharing it is not to draw out the tragic elements for shock value. The real power comes in the enigmatic way students have identified their key moments and have gained strength from such a terrible and monstrous act.

The Tale of Two Brothers

Once there were two brothers. Being close in age, most times they were best friends, and at other times, irritated enemies. As little ones, they found entertainment in the interests of boys (the sandbox, action figures, and Little League baseball), but as time passed, these two brothers drifted apart as many brothers do. They began to embrace their own distinct ideas and respond to the adventures of the world in their own way.

As with all of us, there comes a time when the choices we make become solely our responsibility. The seemingly trivial choices made for us when we are young fall right in our laps, and it's up to us to take action. What clothing will we wear? What kinds of people will we associate with? These two brothers were now faced with the opportunity to make the choices that would define their lives.

As adolescents, the brothers were confronted with a barrage of ideas that in their critical seconds of self-talk and individual thought would have a dramatic effect on their development as adults. Everywhere we look we are faced with the challenges that these two brothers endured. The TV, the Internet, the media—it all squares up on us like a schoolyard bully and demands that we face our greatest fears.

The first brother in our story (we'll refer to him as "the confused brother") begins his journey where most of us start making decisions on our own: junior high school. This brother discovered how wonderful it felt to have his independence. He loved going places on his own and meeting friends of his own temperament. He enjoyed the freedom of exploring all the things he found interesting. He was extremely smart and savvy, and this allowed him to make friends with people older than himself and to get involved in the vices of young adults. Being attractive and physically fit allowed this brother to gain employment doing jobs that are usually assigned to older kids. The adventure of becoming an adult got more exciting each day. However, this brother misjudged the playing field and mistakenly fell for some old tricks that we all must be aware of. These mistakes were based in the false beliefs that so many youth fall prey to.

The Big Three Fatal Beliefs

These are not the only mistaken beliefs young people have, but they are the potentially fatal ideas that advertisers dish out to a vulnerable age group. Tightly interwoven into the fabric of this period in life are the notions that lead

> If there is a dollar to be made on the identities of teenagers, someone will sell them.

young people to act on their own behalf. If these deeply seated misconceptions were debunked, there wouldn't be as much money to be made. You may think that I'm witch hunting right now, but trust me, if there is a dollar to be made on the identities of teenagers, someone will exploit them. Once these messages are programmed into the young, they can easily be led to the cash registers to buy. Here they are:

1. **The idea that our teen years are the most important and fun time we will ever experience.** Although these years are formative and unique, they are inherently just an emergent process. They are the brief awakening of the infant potential within all of us. Everyone should enjoy being young, but we should also recognize that a larger story is unfolding, and we'll never see it in its fullness if we are hypnotized into believing this is the climax of the tale.

2. **The idea that teenagers are entitled to a negligent and irresponsible period in their lives.** It has become a birthright to be able to shirk the duties that are connected to adulthood. In many instances, we have pried

the door open for injury and harm and have justified our actions with the age group we belong to. A willful ignorance has invaded the brains of teens who believe there is god-given virtue to having fun at others' expense.

3. **The idea that adults are out of touch and irrelevant to the lives of youth.** Never before has there been such a marginalization of our elders. The message that your teen years should be unadulterated by the influence of adults is a divide-and-conquer attack on wisdom. This lie is the message that adults are the stupid and neurotic comic relief on your grand stage. Once this misconception is embedded in the minds of the young, they are totally disconnected from anyone who has lived through this difficult developmental stage. They are not only removed from the most vested and dedicated forces in their lives, but they are also girded with a stubborn shield of self-entitlement.

The confused brother was entranced with these ideas to the extent that counterperspectives were completely unsettling. Month by month and year by year, this brother immersed himself so deeply into his murky self-image that nothing maintained its sanctity. A casual sexual experience seemed regular; drug use, mandatory; and devotion to the ignorant like minds around him, a sworn oath. Slowly this confused brother lost the critical distance necessary for evaluating himself. The mirror of his conscience was so distorted that the reflections of his words and actions became degenerate and vulgar. His ideas about progress and success became intertwined with hopelessness. His journey and adventure could not be penetrated by anyone who truly loved him. This confused brother was controlled by the same forces we see active upon students today. He was enamored with his own story line. His paradigm became the drama that he worked so hard to create. Soon, this lifestyle perpetuated itself.

The other brother (we'll call him the brother with clarity) sought to understand some of the deeper virtues of life. He faced all the same temptations but could identify his confused brother's weakness. This brother decided at a young age that he would not fall victim to the ravages of confusion and failure. He enjoyed the privilege of having relationships with the adults who cared for him. He was not manipulated into thinking he needed any of the accoutrements of pop culture. He did not find meaning in pop fashion or pop music or any other temporary mindset. Through clarity and guidance, this brother found a path that was exciting and different. He connected with people, and his critical seconds built a powerful vision for his later life.

Freshman, sophomore, junior, and senior years in high school slipped freely through the confused brother's fingers. Each year a pseudosavvy

> If you only aspire to be a jackass, after five years, you will only be a very skilled jackass.

grew within his soul. Long years of manipulating the truth and living inside excuses and lies created a distorted identity in which negative experiences were the promotions up a hierarchy of hate. To state it plainly, there is no greatness to "being in the game." If you only aspire to be a jackass, after five years, you are only a very skilled jackass. The only people who will respect a long-standing commitment to systematically choking the artistry out of one's life are those who benefit from your creative death.

At twenty years old, the confused brother's life would reach a darkened wood. Some people may analyze just one facet of the story to try to find an explanation. They'd look for one specific cause. In retrospect, it was all of the little seconds of choice invested into this young man's confusion that ultimately delivered his destiny.

Along with another confused young man (they really couldn't be called friends), the confused brother began a series of life-changing seconds. First, he gained access to a gun. It seemed only fitting that he should protect his image with a firearm. He didn't see that the strength of his character should never need to be physically defended; it is undeniable and inarguable if it is noble. Next, the pair of youth, bound by the facade of gang association, stole a car—a red two-seated sports car perfect for attracting the profound kind of trouble these two were drawn to. They were so blind that their brief and secret thrill ride only now stands out as an obvious lesson. As they sped along the freeway in their stolen entertainment, they happened along a small imported truck traveling slow and carefully. Maybe it was the speed of the driver in the truck, or maybe it was just pent-up aggression, but the predatory nature of these confused young men was awakened. An altercation unfolded right there on the freeway. The two vehicles careened in and out of traffic as the young men screamed obscenities to escalate the intensity. The brother in our story unholstered the .25-caliber Jennings semiautomatic pistol in one last attempt to trump the driver of the truck. In coolheaded premeditation, the brother directed his driving accomplice from the passenger's seat. These were his exact words:

"Slow down, man. Pull up on the passenger's side." The driver did as he was told. "Lean back," the brother said. He reached the gun across his friend's view and nearly out the driver's-side window. Gunshots rang out.

The bullets did not hit the driver of the truck. The glass in the cab window shattered, and one of the shots struck the passenger. The whole incident lasted no longer than a few seconds. Jennifer Montgomery, a nineteen-year-old girl, went out with her husband that day and never returned home. A bullet struck her in the side of the head, just an inch above her ear. She slumped over in her husband's lap, bleeding to death. She was six months pregnant.

At that moment, the young brother in the stolen car became no longer confused. In a moment of clarity, he saw in crisp lucidity the magnitude of his choices. Later, he'd recall, "I saw the glass shatter, and I saw the girl's head jerk to the side, and I saw blood, and I knew…I just hurt someone."

In those critical seconds, the lesson dawned on this brother: we all have to live in the world we create with our choices. It

> We all have to live in the world that we create with our choices.

was a paralyzing consciousness, and it crashed down on this young man's mind. The two sped away, intent on escaping the impending consequences. They ditched the gun, which they had broken into pieces in hopes that the weapon could not prove their guilt. They ditched the car and wiped away as many fingerprints as they could, missing a few. They fled into hiding with the slim hope that the girl in the truck would recover. Their hopes were in vain.

Jennifer Montgomery died. Her baby died. Over the next few days, the city was abuzz with the story of the "freeway killers." In a tearful plea, Jennifer's husband, Ricky (the driver), cried to the public to find justice. For three days, the whole state of Arizona stood still while every news outlet reported the story. A gigantic manhunt encompassed the state, and the search drew inward on the hiding fugitives. This is where the tale breaks from the predictable story line of gangsta-rap crime. No shoot-out took place with the police. No stolen airplane came out of nowhere to fly the young brother off to a foreign country. Along with the gun and the car, the police made short work of solving the crime and found the brother. He was taken into custody as he was trying to flee the state hiding in the trunk of a car. In court, there was no mercy. He was sentenced to life in prison with a sixty-five-year minimum.

At this very moment, this critical second, we could go to an Arizona State prison and see this confused brother living in a six-by-eight cell, where he'll stay for the rest of his life. His critical seconds define him to this day. Buried and forgotten deep in the bowels of a concrete nightmare, he will not be before the parole board until he is eighty-five years old.

This is not where the story ends. The other brother embraced clarity as a young man. He embarked on a heart-pounding adventure and discovered an extraordinary secret that he shares with others. The secret is the critical seconds of brilliance that lie dormant in every person's heart. It is in knowing that one can act upon the opportunities that life presents. This brother makes his choices from a position of confidence, with love as his guiding force. I know all of this because this brother is me. My brother Nghia is the confused brother. I watched him throughout our lives make choices that defined him in his critical seconds.

The lessons to be learned here are not only the obvious warnings against guns and gangs. Most of the people I share this story with are not into gangs or prone to violence. The response I get most often is the attitude

> If we could feel the excruciating emotional pain that our loved ones feel when we fail, we would work harder to preserve *their* well being.

that says, "I like doing my own thing, but I won't hurt anyone else." If you look closely, the crimes committed against Jennifer Montgomery were only the beginning. I wasn't there, so I didn't see this, but my stepmother relayed the incident. My father sat down in his chair to watch the news, and there the face of his son flashed up on the screen as the headline read, "Wanted: The Freeway Murderer." The media was brutal when the story first broke. The headlines called my brother a "maniac" and a "psychopath." At first, the story was relayed as a random act of violence. Later, the details behind how the two cars were really fighting clarified the actual events in court. My stepmother described the look of horror and shock that came across my father's face. She said he stood up from his chair, walked into his bedroom, collapsed on his bed, and wept. The strongest most stoic and unemotional man I've ever known cried as the devastating story began to sink in. I, too, have shed tears. In contemplation of what the Montgomery family has lost, I've hurt privately with them. Still, in all candor, I have to admit that the most lingering pain I've experienced is seeing the brokenheartedness of my parents. They elected to appear on our local news and apologize for the actions of their son. They wore the disgrace and responsibility publicly and never shied from Nghia as their son. The penetrating one-second awakening we glean from this story is that every one of us is surrounded by people who will be deeply affected by our actions. When we're young, we just can't see how making selfish choices isn't an independent act. If we could feel the excruciating emotional pain that our loved ones feel when we fail, we would work harder to preserve *their* well-being.

Identity Crisis

My brother represents so many students around this country. They're hopelessly searching for significance through the fleeting garments of pop culture. It's sad to see my brother's current condition. It's not that prison has been hard physically on him; he doesn't have tattoos or scars from prisonyard fights. None of the stereotypical characteristics fit his description. Nghia is bright and well mannered; he has startling intelligence and exquisite penmanship. When people ask me if I really think pop culture had an influence on him, I answer, most definitely! No one can convince me that this sharp middle-class kid is a bad apple. He was targeted as a consumer and led step-by-step through the buying process. In a desperate attempt to find his identity, he walked straight into his commercially fabricated "deathstyle." The confusion we all feel at times in our lives should never make us so deluded. We're lulled into thinking that all the stuff we see on television is meaningless and has no repercussions. I'm not assigning blame. I know my brother made his own choices, and that is what I try to convince others about of themselves. Every day that you live, whether you realize it or not, you're creating yourself.

As I recount the story here at my computer, I'm still shaken from the memories it resurrects. So many people's lives changed in an instant, even mine. I've been asked many times over the years how I decided to use the story for a positive message. People believe that I made the choice to reach students because of this terrible tragedy. Here lies a powerful truth concerning my commitment to students. When I was first informed of the manhunt for my brother in Arizona, I was in Pennsylvania, speaking in schools. I had decided years before that my truest fulfillment was in motivating students. I didn't manipulate the story of my brother's crimes into speaking engagements. At this writing, it has been fourteen years since he was sentenced; this is the first written account of the circumstances surrounding his choices. To be forthright, I admit that the press coverage helped to open some doors when the story was new, but my rap album and youth ministry were bigger priorities. I did not begin full-time professional speaking until late 1999, nine years after the story broke.

So how do you do it? How do you maintain clarity for your moments of brilliance? How do you not only make right choices but

> If you really want to ingrain an awesome habit into your life; you must discipline your passions.

make great choices? The following advice comes from a person who has analyzed every year of his late teens and twenties, looking for the secrets. In this process, I have uncovered the hidden wisdom of finding yourself without killing yourself. Throughout reading this book, you may have already identified some of your powerful seconds, and you may have already taken action, but if you really want to ingrain an awesome habit into your life, you must discipline your passions. It doesn't make a difference where you were born, how much money you have, if you're short or tall, or if you're great looking or not so great looking; if you take dominion over the passions that drive you, you will be successful at whatever you do. This is especially important for youth who don't have strong parental examples. Even if your parents aren't the best role models, you can learn the skills it takes to be disciplined. In my adult life, I encounter people every day who have yet to find the power of self-mastery. The best starting place is in your self-talk. A verbal affirmation can be a powerful means for determining your direction. So I created a cheat sheet to developing a winning frame of mind for beginners. It is composed of promises made to oneself. Commit these promises to memory and watch how they change your state of mind.

Promise 1: I will practice the skill of critical thinking every day. Nothing in pop culture is to be internalized. I will analyze everything I am told and only act when I know I have credible information.

Promise 2: I will document my thoughts and dreams and look to my innate wisdom to guide me. Through blogs, a journal, or a diary, I will catalogue my ideas for future reference. I will commit myself to the passionate search for my purpose and my voice and will operate within them when they are found.

Promise 3: I will adopt standards of excellence for all of my relationships. Whether romantic or platonic, I will recognize the beauty of the journey. I will find friendships that reinforce my dignity and perpetuate a benevolent direction. I will only align myself with people who assist me in making a statement of greatness with my life.

Promise 4: I will prioritize my health and intelligence as critical components for experiencing life. I will glorify knowledge as an empowering tool, and I will prepare my body to skillfully bear it. I will empower my enabled spirit by preparing my mind and body for the gift of love and service.

Promise 5: I will identify my critical seconds of brilliance and will confidently act upon them. I will recognize split-second opportunities as the gateways to my destiny. I will use my intuitive and compassionate self to better the circumstances of others.

Chapter Summary

Can you identify some of the sources of bad information that young people are exposed to?

Clarity often comes to us through tragedy. Have there been any moments of clarity that have taught you lessons that were born out of terrible circumstances?

Give examples: _____

_____

_____

What times of the day could you recite the affirmative promises?

What are some of the ways you discipline your passions?

If the story told in this chapter relayed the tale of your sibling, what would you have done?

Chapter 11

The Blink of an Eagle's Eye

All our dreams can come true, if we have the courage to pursue them.

Walt Disney

If you work in leadership for any length of time, you've experienced the utter joy of succeeding as well as the complete frustration of failing. Leadership is much like parenting. As a parent, I'm constantly startled at how emotionally involved I am with my kid's development. Since my sons Jaden and Adam were born, I find I am more prone to cry at stories that pertain to kids. Every day as an entrepreneur, I ride the roller coaster of owning a business. I sense my father's contributions seasoning my daily life without even being aware of it. My wife and I are more connected than ever before through the experience of parenting. We are also confronted with the challenges of running a business and maintaining her career. We find this period very joyful and scary at the same time. It's funny how the beginning of this new-found anxious paranoia happens. It started when my wife, Lori, was pregnant. It continues through the raising of our sons and evolves every day so that I never get used to it. It's this underlying fear of making a mistake that compels me to write this chapter. Some of the suggestions expressed here are simply thought provoking, but others are more pointed. Being a parent, being self-employed, and working with youth for over fifteen years now has forced me to examine these ideas in depth. May they assist you in your journey.

Don't Sacrifice Yourself

Bill Maher skillfully works the phrase "It's for the children" into his comedy act. He lampoons the notion that any manner of political agenda may be justified by using the well-being of "the children" in rhetoric. Limit freedom of speech—for the children's sake. Limit civil rights—to protect the younger generation's morality. The comedy in these jokes comes from how valid this observation is. For too long, people have used "the children" to cloak their selfish agendas. This is the reason I believe that we as adults should commit more fully to enriching our own lives.

Without strong individual visions, there is no example of development for our students. In this accelerating culture, successful mentoring will come from those who can and have navigated the reality of living. Kids will naturally be more adept than we are at navigating the technological environment

> The most profound individuality comes from critical thought and that is the source of what is missing in our world: authenticity.

in which we are raising them. Will their ease in the new age be helpful or destructive? There is no such thing as the "good old days," and in many cases there is no real concept of "traditional family values." The young families raising children today have to contend with the information-age education their children are exposed to. These facts make it imperative that parents model a functional life trajectory based on today's challenges. We must not give up *our* critical seconds of brilliance to help our kids grow up. Moms, do not be manipulated into giving up a professional career "for their sake." This would be like mother tigers giving up crucial hunting skills in order to raise their cubs by a set of rules that the hunters dictated, whereby they convince the mother tiger that *her* mother didn't have to do distasteful and irresponsible tasks such as providing. Absurd, isn't it? The reality I want you to see is that there is a profit motive in manipulating you with your insecurities about not being a good parent, teacher, or leader. Parents, if you have the luxury of being able to stay home with your kids during their formative years, commit them to exemplifying your personal ambitions in projects of your own. The most profound individuality comes from critical thought, and that is the source of what is missing in our world: authenticity. Our children hunger for this more than ever before.

The Excitement of Potential

There is a time in all of our lives when we feel the excitement of the direction in which we are headed. The butterflies flutter in our hearts when we think of the possibilities. An underlying momentum of enthusiasm carries us through our day. One of the most sobering lessons is learned when we are let down by the outcome—all of that uncomfortable excitement, just to be devastated in the end. Wisdom, in many instances, is defined by one's ability to not get overly excited. People begin to sculpt their perspectives around the times they were disappointed, rather than getting addicted to the pleasure

> Your peak experience is not only dependent on exacting a brilliant idea on mankind; it is also executing a brilliant recovery following a failure.

of success. In every situation, they begin the arduous process of deflating everyone's hopes in the spirit of "keeping it real." Constantly scrutinizing the details, these people will point out the challenges as they arise. They will explain to everyone why ideas and visions shouldn't be trusted and how they were burned once when they dreamed for a moment.

We all encounter momentary obstacles. It's the critical seconds that follow our defeats that get us back moving in the right direction. Your peak experience is not only dependent on exacting a brilliant idea on mankind; it is also dependent on executing a brilliant recovery following failure. To create a habit of winning is to *train* as though you will most likely overcome. One second of resilience can enable you to bounce back from a setback and succeed in the future.

Training for Performance

Our body gives us a great example of this. When I was in high school, most of the boys took weights as a PE elective. We went into the weight room for fifty minutes a day and got pumped up. Many a scrawny arm graced the mirrors of that gym class. I remember seeing the posing and flexing and attempts to prove one's maturity by counting chest hairs (and then there were the boys!). One of the measures of manhood was the bench press. This exercise is done by lying flat on a bench and lifting weights on both sides of a long bar up off of your chest. "How much you bench, man?" was the question young boys asked each other to prove their strength. For many years following high school, I still bench-pressed in the gym as a usual part of my routine. This continued until I started working out with a personal trainer.

At first, Todd, my personal trainer, began with numerous exercises I had never seen. Day after day I wondered when I'd get to show off a little and bench-press (thinking about it now, I doubt he'd be impressed).

One day I blurted, "can I bench-press now?"

Todd looked at me funny for a second and then said, "Why? What do you need to lift off your chest?"

I couldn't answer because I'd never thought of it that way. For close to twenty years, I just did what had become a habit. Todd explained to me some interesting information. He had been a division-one wrestler for Iowa State University, and he had his bachelor's degree in sports studies and multiple training certifications. Being an expert on human performance and movement, he demonstrated how the human body responds to exercise by adapting to the stimulus provided by the intensity and range of motion. Put simply, my chest muscles were sure to get stronger if I bench-pressed. However, making my body adapt to that movement did nothing to help me enhance my performance in the activities I love, like basketball or racquetball. In fact, unless I was going to walk around with my belly to the floor and my hands out in front of me, bench-pressing was a totally unnatural movement.

Todd explained how he had seen hundreds of misguided weightlifters working endless hours to develop their chests. After years of bench-pressing,

> The truest definition of wisdom is not *observing* a lot of experiences; it is knowing how to get better from all of your experiences.

these people would have the most spectacular pectoral muscles but would also be more prone to injury (due to the fact that most would not work a counter movement), and their well-developed chest muscles would draw their posture out of alignment.

Many of us take our past experiences and misapply their lessons in the context of the present. If we want our critical seconds to benefit us, we must train our minds for performance. Rather than using the same old routines of yesterday, we have to identify our seconds of success and incorporate them into our actions every day. Many people are mentally bench-pressing all the time. They work very hard, and they're getting stronger, but their performance isn't improving. What I mean is that they show up, they go through the motions, and they are recognized for longevity and consistency, but they are continuously learning the wrong lesson. The truest definition of wisdom is not accumulating a lot of experiences; it is knowing how to *get better* from all of your experiences.

Eight Lethal One-Second Habits

When we draw attention to these idiosyncrasies in our behavior, it's easy to pinpoint exactly where our weaknesses are. If we could follow everyone around with a video camera, we would see for ourselves the unconscious habits that we reinforce every day. Take some time to look deeply at your worst habits. You'll see that most of our worst behavior enters the world from our mouths. Shine the spotlight on them, and just like cockroaches, they will scurry away in one second.

1. **Jumping to conclusions.** Some people get the biggest kick out of assuming they know all the information. There's an old adage that shows us the folly of assumption. Take the word "assume" and break it down for the proper definition. When we assume, we make an *ass* out of *u* and *me*.

2. **Blurting.** The tongue has been likened to a match that starts a great fire, and to a rudder that guides a huge ship. In our interactions with people, the wrong word, even an honest word, can change the whole dynamic of a relationship in one second.

3. **Striking things/people.** In one second you can damage people or property in a manner that cannot be repaired. When you are frustrated, if your first inclination is to strike someone or something, you have a serious problem and need to get counseling.

4. **Gossiping.** The love of hearsay and speculation is a dirty habit to form. It is the equivalent of halitosis of the brain. To engage in even one second of gossip is to initiate a reciprocal process by which *you* are now eligible to be the subject of tomorrow's lies and scandal.

5. **Complaining.** Ninety-nine percent of the time, complaining never affects a situation's outcome. The complainer believes that the 1 percent of the time when someone listens and changes things in their behalf justifies the millions of wasted seconds endlessly voicing everything that's wrong in the world. Meanwhile, everyone around the complainer dies a thousand agonizing deaths, praying for the day that the complainer finally shuts up.

6. **Slang cursing.** Four-letter words are the lazy man's communication style. They have no real purpose other than to stroke the curser's ego. To incorporate slang expletives into one's brilliant seconds of poetry only cheapens the value of your words. Most great communicators never use slang unless they are caught in a careless moment. Eliminate this habit from your discourse and master the long way around with your creative language.

7. **Procrastinating.** Examine procrastination and you will see that it is the blatant misuse of your critical moments of brilliance. The time that you invest in putting off your greatest achievements could be used enjoying the adventure of positive actions. The second that you act upon your ideas and passions is worth hundreds, thousands, or

maybe even millions of dollars. When you procrastinate, you are walking right up to the trash can and throwing your best away.

8. **Assigning blame.** When we fail to take responsibility for our actions, we stand out as though there is a large booger on our upper lip. Everyone sees it, but no one wants to say anything. So, too, when we assign blame to someone else, this habit begins to stand out as a glaring flaw. When we are asked to give an account for our actions, we experience a pivotal second in which blame can rest anywhere. Let it rest on you as a habit, and watch how your influence grows.

Those are some of the nasty split-second habits that will bear a huge impact on your ability to lead. Now, here are some of the awesome seconds that help you create an epic saga of masterpiece moments. Make these your habits.

Six Stunning Masterpiece Moments

1. **Discernment.** Like balance or equilibrium, this is a mental skill that must be honed to an acute perfection. People are all naturally endowed with an innate wisdom that guides their judgment. Discernment will help us achieve an inner consensus for all decisions. Practice reflecting on solutions that arise from your gut feeling. Make it your habit to find resolutions that reinforce your discerning intuitions.

2. **Manners.** These subtle punctuations to our everyday routines are the delicate brushstrokes of our masterpiece moments. Injecting "please" and "thank you" into your vocabulary will have immediate positive results. Make manners a one-second habit today, and experience the higher levels of class and influence.

3. **Gentle Kindness.** Kindness is a state of being of the same sort as manners. Gentleness is defined as strength under control. A gentle way shows a refined intellect. To adopt this habit is to proclaim a deep security within yourself. Your recognition of the beauty and sophistication that binds us all together enables others to blossom.

4. **Affection.** The many perversions of physical affection have skewed our perceptions when it pertains to our demeanor. To show affection is a sign of perpetual appreciation for others. To compliment, hug, give "dabs" (bump knuckles), high five, and in certain appropriate situations give a respectful kiss shows a deep social awareness. These moments communicate a generous and approachable heart.

5. **Gratitude.** Every day of our lives is a gift we have been given and an opportunity to experience a new reality. To acknowledge this in our actions takes premeditation and practice. All of the momentary struggles we face today gain importance when we remove the assurance that we will face anything at all tomorrow. Gratitude loves all of

life. It is welcoming the difficult for the sake of its being a part of the saga.

6. **Thoughtfulness.** This is the focused execution of the first five stunning moments. You must develop an addiction to your creative ideas. If you let them improve those around you, you will enter knowledge of the most mind-blowing high. Start thinking of ways to use your unique voice and personality to get involved with life like you've never thought possible. Aim your energy toward sculpting thoughtful actions from everyday opportunities.

Chapter Summary

Have you planned out personal ambitions for your life?

Can you think of how your failures have helped you succeed with new insight?

Have you ever struggled with one of the eight lethal one-second habits?

How did you finally overcome the habit?

How are your critical moments becoming a masterpiece?

Chapter Twelve

The Artistry of Your Critical Moments

Let your heart guide you. It whispers, so listen closely.

The Land Before Time

When you encounter greatness for one second in your life, you'll never want to settle for anything less. As more of your world takes shape under the carefully crafted chisel of your choices, your artistry will awe those who observe you. It all boils down to just one second. The second of impulse, the second of thought, the second of choice—these can be managed and controlled. Impulse management will set the stage for your critical moments of brilliance. Identifying which direction you should focus your impulses begins a powerful creative process. Once you've directed your impulses, your brain will take over, and your thoughts will begin the process of engineering your dreams. Linger all day in your thoughts of beauty and inspiration. Immerse yourself in the oasis of your ideas. Take special pride in this unique capacity inside you. The actions that flow from this contemplative state will be forged forever on the people who are changed by your brilliance. You'll sense the purpose that comes from these seconds when they are guided by love.

To get our best and most life-changing moments to begin, my advice is always the same: you must make a choice. The choice is to wastefully love with your life. This means that you should never be stingy with your desire to give of yourself. I wish I could tell you that all of your dreams would happen overnight. Unfortunately, the race is a marathon, not a sprint. This journey will be a lifelong quest to discover the beauty and passion locked inside the soul of mankind. So, if you're serious about feeling a rush beyond any other thrill, it starts when you make the first big choice from your heart; you must choose to volunteer.

At eighteen years old, I was open to anything. I had started a rap band and toured the country, and I had even graduated from high school. What other possible thrill could I uncover? I taunted those around me, "I'll do anything!" One special lady took me up on my challenge.

Sharon Henning is a classy Scottsdale, Arizona, socialite. She has always rubbed shoulders with the well-to-do crowd, and she knows her way around the rich. She has an unwavering gaze and always looks immaculate from head to toe. Despite her sophisticated disposition, Sharon has headed the senior care ministry for my family's church for close to two decades. It was she who invited me to participate in the most daunting task yet: the nursing home. Before a group of teenage volunteers, Sharon took me up on my taunting challenge. She began briefing us on the "blessing" we were to experience with the senior citizens. I was passionate about helping people, and this seemed like a piece of cake. In my mind I pictured a bunch of grandmas and grandpas. Little did I know I was about to face some of the deepest possible reflections of the human spirit.

On Wednesday afternoon, we got all the young volunteers together for a visit to the care facility. As we arrived, I wanted to show the others that I was all ready for this ministry, and I quickly jumped out of the van. I walked right up to the front entrance and threw the door open. As I drew in a breath to exclaim, "Hello, old folks!" an unfamiliar aroma struck my nostrils. I stopped dead in my tracks and slapped my hand over my nose. It smelled like four-day-old pee and green beans. My impulse was to leave immediately. My mind screamed at me, "I can't do this!" Another little voice reminded me, "You chose love." Taking control of my fearful (and a little grossed out) impulses, I proceeded. The first person I encountered was a staff member from the facility. He looked at me and asked, "Are you one of the volunteers?" I nodded my head. "Good!" he said and walked me over to a room. "There's a guy in there, and he's dying. Go keep him company." I was shocked! "Well, what if he dies while I'm in there?" The staff member informed me that the patient had advanced lung cancer and had only a short time left. Probably not today, and maybe not tomorrow, but he was going to pass soon.

I slowly entered the room. I could see that the man had oxygen being fed into his nose through a tube. I looked at his chart at the edge of the bed. His name was Wesley. He didn't move. "Great…he's dead already," I thought to myself. "Um, Hi, Wesley, my name is Leon. Um, I love you….Don't die?" I had no clue what to say to this guy. Wesley looked up at me and began to speak. He seemed happy that I was there, and he started making an effort to tell me about his life through labored breathing.

As our conversation began, I thought to myself, "I can do this." Just then, another young volunteer walked into the room. For some reason, this didn't set well with Wesley. In his old-man way, he freaked out! "You!" he pointed at the startled volunteer. "Get out!" He looked at me. "You…I like you; you stay." "Ha ha, my old guy likes me!" My mind snapped back to reality, and I wondered if I had said that out loud. Luckily, it was only in my head, and the other volunteer left. Wesley and I talked for a little longer, and then he said, "You know what would be really nice?" I looked right in his eyes and saw a glimmer of cheer. In this poor man's last days here on earth, I figured he was entitled to some sort of pleasantry. "Anything, Wesley," I snapped back. "If you could put me in the wheelchair and roll me around?" Now, I wasn't trained for that sort of thing, but I was eighteen and didn't know any better. "OK!" Without a second thought, I reached over and grabbed the oxygen off of his face. I lifted his weakened body out of the bed and into the wheelchair. He started breathing very heavily and wheezing loudly. Coming to my scary senses, I asked, "Are you all right?" He nodded his head. I mumbled, "OK, I love you….Don't die." I was 75 percent sure we would be fine. At eighteen, 75 percent chances are good enough. I wheeled Wesley through the halls and out onto an outdoor patio. The sun was shining, the grass was green, and I proudly affirmed to myself, "I'm glad I chose love."

We talked a little longer, and time sort of stopped for a while. Wesley told me how he had been a construction worker and how he had built houses. He told me how he had relatives, but none would come and visit him in these final days.

Then, without warning, Wesley grew serious and looked me in the eye. "Thank you. I can't tell you how much I appreciate you. I want to give you something." He started to take off his watch. He held his old watch out to me. "Here, you can have it. I have some money, too. You can have it all!" I was dumbfounded. "I could never take a gift like that," I stammered. *Did he just say money?* I wavered for a moment, almost asked, and then thought better of it. "OK," I said and took the watch.

So, needless to say, I was totally blown away. This guy was dying, and he wanted to give me a gift. Not just a gift, but he had probably given me one of his only remaining possessions. I was touched. Without knowing what to say, I hugged Wesley. Weakly, he hugged me back.

We could probably end the story there and get a wonderful lesson from Wesley's act of generosity. Many readers are probably thinking to themselves, "Let's go to the nursing home. The old people will give us stuff!" Wouldn't it be easy to choose love in *that* split second? Well, the real lesson was yet to come.

There we were, basking in the glow of newfound friendship, when Wesley looked up at me and said, "I have to urinate." I couldn't hide the fact that this caught me off guard. I started thinking out loud, "What do I do?" "Take me to the bathroom!" he said. Wesley seemed a little annoyed. For all he knew, I had been trained to care for him this way. My brain was racing, and without a second thought, I wheeled him into the closest room.

In every room there was a bathroom. This restroom was the standard hospital sort, with a big hydraulic hinge that closes the door automatically. In we went, and the door shut behind me. It was here that I remembered my inner conflict and became aware of impulse management. I began to realize where I was. The door was closed, the old man was waiting, and there was the toilet. I took inventory of my situation. Then it dawned on me. In an instant, I knew what I was expected to do. "Oh no! I'm not doing that!" ranted my inner dialogue. "You chose love," said a fainter but clear voice. Wesley said he had to do number one (I hope all my readers know the number system). I calculated the risk silently, "*I've done number one. Number one is the easy number.*"

Acting against my impulse to leave him there, I reached down and helped Wesley out of his chair. He reached up his arms and clasped his hands around my neck for support. I shuffled around and hovered above the toilet. Here was the moment of truth. I took down his pants. Amid my revulsion and embarrassment, I turned away. "Please hurry," I thought. There is really no way to write this in a tasteful fashion. Wesley said he had to go number one, but he didn't have any control. He went number two, three, and four! He started crying in humiliation and indignation. I could see the helplessness in his face, so I began to comfort him. "It's all right, Wesley. Don't worry about it." He calmed down. Then it hit me. Wesley couldn't do anything for himself—not anything! Being too weak from the cancer in his body, Wesley could not perform the most elementary task, the task we've all known how to do since we were small children.

"You chose love," my inner voice softly reminded. I had a choice to make. We all have a choice to make. You see, when you decide that you want to manage your impulses, you will quickly see how hard it is to be guided by love. You're probably thinking, "Is this Chinese flower power?" I'm not talking about hippie love. I'm talking about the kind of love that makes you visualize beyond yourself. There exists a kind of love that makes you regard others' needs as more important than your own. It's this kind of gritty, real, tactile love that makes a difference in the world.

I reached for the toilet paper. I'm not talking about two little squares, either. I needed the *whole roll*. I'll spare you the details, but I did it. I cleaned that old man up, put him back in the chair, and wheeled him out. I quickly dismissed myself and went back to where the volunteers were meeting. Each volunteer seemed to have a story that detailed his or her willingness to sacrifice for the cause. I would hear none of them. Nothing could have been worse than my story.

"I ain't never goin' back!" I pouted. One of the other volunteers told me how an old lady with a walker had solicited his help. She asked if he would tie her shoe. He obliged, and when he bent down to tie the shoelace, she peed on his hand. Even that was not as horrific as *my* nursing-home tale. When I shared my experience, everyone agreed. Many of the volunteers could not stop laughing; I was not amused. The magnitude of choosing to allow love to guide my impulses was more than I was willing to bear. I swore to myself I would never go back to the nursing home.

Over the next week, I began hearing that quiet little voice more often. It gently nagged me with the choice I had so arrogantly made. As I reflected on my actions, I recalled how much I wanted to make a difference in the world. The quiet and reassuring voice explained that great leadership is not always glamorous or convenient. It explained that timeless influence enters the world humbly and with poise. Most of all, it whispered the invitation to true significance very convincingly to my heart and mind. It was one of the most difficult decisions I've ever made, but the following week, I went back to the nursing home. The week after that, I went again. The week after that, I went twice. Not only did I visit the care center with the volunteers, but I also went on my own time. In the subsequent weeks, I poured myself into my relationship with Wesley. We talked and spent time just hanging out. On some occasions, I sensed he was a little cloudy about who I was, but he was always appreciative. That eighty-five-year-old man became something special to me. He was more than an errand to run or a charity case; Wesley was my friend.

I still remember the day I went rushing into his room, saying, "Hi Wesley!" I was greeted by an empty bed with only a pile of sheets folded neatly in the center. I frantically called the nearest staff member. "Nurse, where did you move Wesley?" The nurse only shook her head, and the realization

> Respect is the intense personal acknowledgement that our world is bigger than we know and that we are all connected within it.

that Wesley had passed began to hit me. In his final days among the living, Wesley could have passed into eternity with empty bitterness for the world. He died alone in a rest home. None of his relatives would come to visit him. I never asked Wesley what events or sad dynamic created such a rift in his personal life. I guess I really didn't want to know. Instead, Wesley allowed me to catch a quick glimpse of the purest definition of respect. It's the intense personal acknowledgment that our world is bigger than we know and that we are all connected within it. This was the beginning of my recognition of my critical moments.

It's been said that in the seconds before you die, your whole life passes before your eyes. You see all the good times and the bad. You see the romance and the passion. You see your friends and family, your homes and the places you love. I have moments like this all the time. Sometimes, when I go into my bedroom, I look through an old box where I keep all of my best stuff—sentimental treasures I've kept close for many years. This box is where I keep that old watch that Wesley gave me. It's scratched and faded, and it doesn't keep time very well (it was in pretty rough shape when he gave it to me), but I'll take that watch out and just stare at it. In those moments, my whole life passes before my eyes. When I look in on my boys before I go to bed, I'm overwhelmed with a simple yet powerful wave of love for them. I see all of their birthdays and holidays, their hobbies and unique personalities. In those moments, my whole life passes before my eyes. When I look into the eyes of every student I've ever spoken to, I see the potential and brilliance they possess, and my whole life passes before my eyes—the life I *want* to live.

Every day, whether you know it or not, you're creating yourself. With every word and with every action, you're adding or subtracting something from your life. Your critical moments of brilliance can either pass you by unnoticed and forgotten, or they can be doorways to a new adventure. The choice is yours.

This chapter wouldn't be complete without a personal acknowledgment to the people who have helped me create some masterpiece moments. A big thank-you to Sharon Henning, a big thank-you to all of the students who have responded to the challenge to choose love, and most of all, thanks, Wesley.

Chapter Summary

Does the term "wastefully love" make sense to you?

Have you ever had to express love in a manner that seemed distasteful?

Give examples: _____

_____

_____

Name the loving relationships in your life that define you.

When your whole life passes before your eyes, what does it look like?

Which relationships make you proud to be a part of them?

Chapter Thirteen

One-Second Execution: "Do or Die"

Not armies, not nations, have advanced the race; but here and there, in the course of ages, an individual has stood up and cast his shadow over the world.

Edwin Hubbell Chapin

It only takes a second to change a perspective. If you watch closely, you'll catch yourself being entertained with news and rumors of all that's happening around you. Living in the commune-style social environment that humans foster cultivates a desire to be aware of the considerable challenges we face. We want to know about the weather and traffic conditions, housing and schools, business and economy. We even want to know all the juicy details about everyone's personal life. For some reason we feel empowered and safe if we are glued to the television and our faces are buried in a newspaper and the Internet, but what do we do with all of the information we consume? Do any of the stories we read in the tabloids ever make any significant difference in the way we behave? If information were a tangible item, our mental storage bins would be overflowing with old and rotten garbage. Just as if we never threw out our kitchen trash, we have become information pack rats. This clutter can keep us from being as effective as we could be if we just cleaned out our mental closets. This mountain of needless information gets in the way of more important decision making.

For so many, the truly pertinent choices in life are clouded with the inane and banal options between the stupid and the meaningless. Start right now and take advantage of the ability to make your own important and defining choices. Look within and dismiss the anxiety that has been exacted upon you. Commit yourself to walking in the humble and reasonable confidence that you are an intuitive and intelligent individual.

Make room for the idea that all advertising (print ads, television, Internet sites, and radio) is someone's attempt to control your choices.

The final chapter of this book serves as a challenge and a warning. The ideas we have explored are more than just good suggestions. They are significant messages of wisdom. Many of these conclusions came with a costly emotional investment. I have shared some of my family's worst tragedies to illustrate my book with authentic subject matter. Now, having spilled my deepest feelings out on paper for you to evaluate, I give you this challenge: judge for yourself. Use the same measure I've encouraged you to use with the world of pop culture on this piece of literature. You should probe intently through the words that have been shared in these pages. In the light of what has been discussed, examine your critical moments. Are you seeing them? Have you uncovered your brilliant, creative, and passionate tendencies?

What's at stake if you choose to be a blind follower? I have interviewed many students who just didn't mind that they were being controlled by someone else. Their rationality was, "I'm having fun, so why does it matter?" Right now, you may not feel an intense desire to buck the system with your ideas, due to the fact that everything seems to be fine. However, mark my words, there comes a time in everyone's life when they question their world. Part of the maturing process is the taking flight of your individual thought life.

In a thousand years, the people of the future will see how the world was shaped by a handful of brilliant thinkers. It will be clear to those who study us in the next age that millions of people deliberately chose to swim in the sea of the mediocre and the unmemorable. Why? It's my belief that most people make a calculated gamble. It's a trade-off between a life that is unexplored yet safe and a fully perceived adventure that includes some risk. The mediocre and safe is a mirage. In this day and age, our global perspective gives us the revealing truth about the dynamics between leaders and followers. As blind followers, we forfeit our freedom to whoever asserts themselves most. You are being targeted. The direction of our world will be shaped by the ideas initiated in this information age. If you allow yourself to be placated with mild pop-culture entertainment, you're destined to a modern-day fate equivalent to that of history's slaves and peasants. Hypnosis is defined as covert suggestive communication to the subconscious mind. Don't fall for it. Don't let anyone define you with stereotypes or labels. Don't allow slick marketing campaigns to dictate your behavior. Your critical moments of brilliance are the lifeblood of your identity. Feed them with knowledge and act on them when they arise. It's been said that it takes a minute to meditate but a second to die. The keys to life and death hang in the balance, and it's you who makes the choice. Take one second to think.

Chapter Summary

Have you taken inventory of your critical moments of brilliance?

Do you see how advertisers try to control you?

Have you started to document your adventure?

Have you discovered your critical moments of brilliance?

Can you identify your moments of clarity?

List your commitment to clarity in your own words: _____

_____

_____

_____

Index

C

D

H

I

978-0-595-35191-6
0-595-35191-3

Printed in the United States
34706LVS00005B/184-435